THE HOLOCAUST

The Holocaust:
The Third Reich and the Jews

DAVID ENGEL

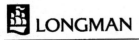 LONGMAN

An imprint of **PEARSON EDUCATION**

Harlow, England · London · New York · Reading, Massachusetts · San Francisco ·
Toronto · Don Mills, Ontario · Sydney · Tokyo · Singapore · Hong Kong · Seoul ·
Taipei · Cape Town · Madrid · Mexico City · Amsterdam · Munich · Paris · Milan

Pearson Education Limited
Edinburgh Gate
Harlow
Essex CM20 2JE
England

and Associated Companies around the world

Visit us on the World Wide Web at
www.pearsoned.co.uk

First published 2000

ISBN 978-0-582-32720-7

British Library Cataloguing-in-Publication Data
A catalogue record for this book is available from the British Library

Library of Congress Cataloging-in-Publication Data
A catalog record for this book is available from the Library of Congress

19
10

Set by 7 in 10/12 Sabon
Printed and bound in Great Britain by 4edge Ltd, Hockley. www.4edge.co.uk

CONTENTS

An introduction to the Series   vii
Note on Referencing System   viii
Note on Place Names   viii
List of Maps   ix
Acknowledgements   x

PART ONE: THE BACKGROUND   1

1. STUDYING THE HOLOCAUST   1
    Genocide and the Issue of Uniqueness   2
    Why Study the Third Reich and the Jews?   3
    Studying the Holocaust Historically   5

2. THE JEWS   7
    Jewish Origins   7
    The Jews in Christian Europe   8
    In Modern Times   10

PART TWO: ANALYSIS   14

3. HITLER, NAZIS, GERMANS, AND JEWS   14
    The Jews in Hitler's World-view   14
    Jews in the Ideology and Programme of Nazism   17
    Jews in German Public Opinion   20
    True Believers and the First World War   22
    Ordinary Men or Ordinary Germans?   24

4. 1933–41 – A TWISTED ROAD?   26
    'Intentionalism' and 'Functionalism'   27
    The State of Documentation   28
    A Step-by-Step Process?   32
    Jewish Policy and Global Strategy   35

5. RESPONDING TO PERSECUTION   38
    Perceiving the Threat   38
    To Leave or Not to Leave?   41
    Communal Leadership: Coping and Resisting   42
    Zionism, German Jewry, and World Jewry   44
    External Obstacles to Emigration   47

6. THE TRANSITION TO KILLING   50
    Why Begin Killing?   51
    The Means of Murder   56
    Organizing the Transports   59

7. RESPONDING TO MURDER   62
    Information and Imagination   62
    Communal Responsibility and Strategies for Survival   66
    The Unofficial Community and Resistance   69
    Local Non-Jewish Leaders and Populations: Opposition and
    Complicity   72
    Beyond the Nazi Realm   77

    PART THREE: ASSESSMENT   81

8. HUMANITY, MODERNITY, AND THE HOLOCAUST   81

    PART FOUR: DOCUMENTS   88

    Chronology   111
    Glossary and guide to characters   115
    Bibliography   125
    Maps   136
    Index   140

AN INTRODUCTION TO THE SERIES

Such is the pace of historical enquiry in the modern world that there is an ever-widening gap between the specialist article or monograph, incorporating the results of current research, and general surveys, which inevitably become out of date. *Seminar Studies in History* are designed to bridge this gap. The series was founded by Patrick Richardson in 1966 and his aim was to cover major themes in British, European and World history. Between 1980 and 1996 Roger Lockyer continued his work, before handing the editorship over to Clive Emsley and Gordon Martel. Clive Emsley is Professor of History at the Open University, while Gordon Martel is Professor of International History at the University of Northern British Columbia, Canada and Senior Research Fellow at De Montfort University.

All the books are written by experts in their field who are not only familiar with the latest research but have often contributed to it. They are frequently revised, in order to take account of new information and interpretations. They provide a selection of documents to illustrate major themes and provoke discussion, and also a guide to further reading. The aim of *Seminar Studies* is to clarify complex issues without over-simplifying them, and to stimulate readers into deepening their knowledge and understanding of major themes and topics.

NOTE ON REFERENCING SYSTEM

Readers should note that numbers in square brackets [5] refer them to the corresponding entry in the Bibliography at the end of the book (specific page numbers are given in italics). A number in square brackets preceded by Doc. [Doc. 5] refers readers to the corresponding item in the Documents section which follows the main text. Terms and main characters marked with an asterisk can be found in the Glossary.

NOTE ON PLACE NAMES

The names of cities given in the text are their official names in the language of the country to which they belonged on 31 August 1939. Hence Wilno instead of Vilnius or Vilna, but Kaunas instead of Kovno. Exceptions have been made for some cities whose names have well-known English forms (Prague, Vienna, Warsaw). Standard English names have been used for all larger political units.

LIST OF MAPS

1   Europe and its Jews, January 1938   136
2   German, Hungarian, and Soviet expansion and the dismemberment
    of Czechoslovakia and Poland, 1938–39   137
3   The Nazi orbit, 1942   138
4   The murder of European Jewry   139

PUBLISHER'S ACKNOWLEDGEMENTS

The publishers would like to thank the Trust Fund for the Publication of the Proceedings of the Eichmann Trial for permission to reproduce extracts from *The Trial of Adolf Eichmann*, May 1961.

PART ONE: THE BACKGROUND

1 STUDYING THE HOLOCAUST

What follows is the story of an encounter between two groups of people: on one hand those who acted on behalf of the German state, its agencies, or its almost 66 million citizens between 30 January 1933 and 8 May 1945; on the other hand the almost 9 million Jews who lived in Germany and the twenty countries of Europe (Austria, Belgium, Bulgaria, Czechoslovakia, Denmark, Estonia, Finland, France, Greece, Hungary, Italy, Latvia, Lithuania, Luxembourg, the Netherlands, Norway, Poland, Romania, the USSR, and Yugoslavia) that were either ruled directly or occupied by Germany or that made a formal alliance with it at any time during that interval. That encounter resulted in the death of about two-thirds of the latter group, in the large majority of cases as a direct result of actions taken by the former.

The 5.8 million Jews who died at German or German-allied hands, mostly during 1941–45, were almost all unarmed civilians who had committed no organized act of aggression against the German state or society and who posed no real threat to their well-being – at least in terms that made sense to reasonable people in the Western world. Yet the leaders of Germany actively sought their deaths. In fact, most of them came to regard the killing of Jews as one of their most important tasks, and from 1941 on they pursued that aim with ruthless vigour. In other words, the story of the encounter between the Third Reich (as the German state was known during almost all of the period in question) and the Jews ultimately became one of premeditated mass murder.

To be sure, this encounter was not the only instance of premeditated mass murder in human history. In fact, it was neither the largest nor proportionally the most extensive case. Estimates of the number of Soviet civilians who died as a result of their government's deliberate actions against them between 1929 and 1950 vary widely, but all vastly exceed the number of Jews killed by the Third Reich [120]. The losses sustained by the Sinti*, Roma, and related peoples (Gypsies) under the Third Reich may also have reached or even exceeded two-thirds of their pre-1933 population in many parts of Europe [50; 69; 166]. Some have argued that perhaps 95 per cent of the indigenous population of North and South America prior to European settlement – anywhere between 50 million and 100 million people – died between the sixteenth and nineteenth centuries because of the determination of Europeans to annihilate them; others have disputed the reasons for this massive loss of life, but they have affirmed its extent [120; 174]. Yet the murder of Europe's Jews during the Second World War seems to have resulted in many more books, articles, and school courses (not to mention public memorials) than have any other occasions of mass killing. Why this special attention?

GENOCIDE AND THE ISSUE OF UNIQUENESS

Some scholars have insisted that concentrating upon the killing of Jews by the Third Reich more than upon the many other victims of mass murder throughout the ages actually impedes understanding of a broader phenomenon, often called 'genocide'*. This term was invented in 1944 by legal scholar Raphael Lemkin*, a Jewish refugee from German-occupied Poland, who, as an adviser to the US War Department, wrote a book entitled *Axis Rule in Occupied Europe* [*Doc. 1*]. Lemkin defined 'genocide' as 'the destruction of a nation or of an ethnic group' [19 *p. 79*]. Later he stated that although he originally coined the word to designate mass German killings of Jews, he eventually realized that not only Jews but members 'of all peoples, religions, and nationalities' had been or could become victims of the same crime [20 *p. 98*]; for 'genocide does not necessarily mean ... mass killings of all members of a nation ... [but] the destruction of essential foundations of the life of national groups' [19 *p. 79*]. Echoing this view, some have contended that the expression 'The Holocaust' ought to refer not only to the encounter between the Third Reich and the Jews but also to 'the horrors that Poles, other Slavs, and Gypsies endured at the hands of the Nazis' [138 *p. 220*]. Others have extended the term to encompass the Third Reich's treatment of homosexuals, the mentally ill or infirm, and Jehovah's Witnesses, speaking of 11–12 million victims of the Holocaust, half of whom were Jews. Still others have employed the word 'holocaust' also when referring to cases of mass murder not perpetrated by the Third Reich [69; 167; 174].

Against this trend, several historians have pointed to certain features of the encounter between the Third Reich and the Jews that, they claim, render it 'unique' among instances of mass murder. Most often, they hold that 'only in the case of Jewry under the Third Reich' did 'a state set out, as a matter of intentional principle and actualized policy, to annihilate physically every man, woman, and child belonging to a specific people' [166 *pp. 19–20*]. They often contrast this 'total murder of every one of the members of a community' with 'a policy of selective murder designed to destroy ... nations as such, but keep most of their members alive to become a Helot working force', which is what they understand by the term 'genocide' [53 *pp. 34–5*]. Their assertion that such a programme was implemented only once in history, against the Jews by the Third Reich, has been challenged, often angrily, by scholars who have discerned a similar drive toward total murder in the Third Reich's treatment of the Sinti and Roma or of the Poles and other Slavic peoples, in the Turkish massacres of Armenians in 1915, or in European actions against the native peoples of the Americas [166]. Although today almost no serious historian denies that the leaders of the Third Reich did indeed hope to kill each and every Jew within their reach, the basic facts of these other cases are still being disputed, and the issue of 'uniqueness' remains one of intense debate.

The strong feelings that often accompany this debate indicate that it involves more than an academic controversy. Some evidently believe that if Jews can be said to have been victims of a type of persecution *sui generis*, they will have a greater claim to special consideration than other peoples who have also suffered horribly from crimes committed against them. In response to this suspicion, some proponents of the 'uniqueness' argument have stressed that they are *'not ...* endorsing the injudicious claim that the Holocaust is *more evil* than alternative occurrences of ... mass death' [120 *p. 31*]. But even without regard to its moral implications, the debate seems somewhat misplaced. All historical events are unique in the sense that they involve distinctive individuals at particular points in time. However, it is difficult to imagine a historical event that does not share at least some characteristics with other events. One can argue about whether the similarities between two sets of events are more significant than the differences between them, but doing so merely begs the question: significant for what purpose?

WHY STUDY THE THIRD REICH AND THE JEWS?

At bottom, the purpose of any study in the humanities is to learn about human beings – how they think, feel, and behave, and why they do as they do. This, then, ought to be the primary reason for studying the encounter between the Third Reich and the Jews. Hence it seems right to ask first of all whether we can learn anything important about human beings (and thus about ourselves) more effectively by exploring the history of that encounter than we could by considering some other story.

One way to answer this question is to examine what people who have confronted that encounter have found to be most noteworthy about it. Sociologist Zygmunt Bauman has written that 'the Holocaust was born and executed in our modern rational society, at the high stage of our civilization and at the peak of human cultural achievement, and for this reason it is a problem ...' [55 p. x]. Indeed, the story of the Third Reich and the Jews has surprised many people because it runs counter to what they might intuitively have expected from a 'modern rational society' like that of twentieth-century Germany. As will become clear in the following pages, the leaders of the Third Reich looked at the world in a way that made no sense to the rest of Western civilization: in particular, they believed that Jews were (literally) not human, that they were actually a pathogen that threatened (again, literally) to destroy all humanity, and that therefore, by killing all Jews, the Third Reich was actually saving the entire human world from mortal danger. As far as the leaders of the Third Reich were concerned, killing Jews was one of the most important reasons for their state's very being, and they devoted considerable resources – scientific, economic, and human – to carrying it out. Yet while the Third Reich was in existence, hardly anyone outside Germany understood that this was so: such thinking, it was believed, might have been possible in earlier times or in other parts of the world still mired in irrational superstition, but not in modern, rational Europe. Only after extensive study did this fundamental feature of the Third Reich become clear to scholars, who had to overcome their most basic assumptions about the effects of modernity upon human beings in order to do so. In other words, studying the Third Reich and the Jews stretches our self-understanding as human beings; it forces us to rethink fundamentally what it means to be human, especially in the modern world.

Perhaps it will eventually be shown and widely agreed that the leaders of the Third Reich (or of another modern state) thought similarly about other peoples. If so, then studying the histories of those peoples' victimization would no doubt serve the same purpose, and those histories would merit the same attention as that presently given to the history of Europe's Jews during the Second World War. Nevertheless, the case of the Third Reich and the Jews offers a wealth of documentation that has been compiled and analysed for over half a century; it is thus at present more easily accessible to students than other similar cases that might exist. In this light, the question of whether the term 'The Holocaust' ought to be restricted to the encounter between the Third Reich and the Jews or extended to encompass other instances of deliberate mass murder becomes insignificant: the phrase can be used however one wishes, but the manner in which it is used has little bearing upon what the encounter between the Third Reich and the Jews stands to teach us about the meaning of modern human existence.

In what follows, 'the Holocaust' will refer, as a convenient shorthand, solely to the systematic mass murder of European Jews by the Third Reich, without prejudging the issue of possible equivalents.

STUDYING THE HOLOCAUST HISTORICALLY

Because it was rooted in a view of the world that seemed so alien to the one that prevailed in the modern West, the Holocaust has often been said to be incomprehensible. The novelist Yehiel De-Nur, a camp survivor who writes under the pseudonym Ka-Tzetnik, has called Auschwitz* 'another planet', where people 'breathed according to different laws of nature' [29, 3 *p. 1237*]. This perception has led many people to claim that the encounter between the Third Reich and the Jews cannot be discussed in the same way that it is possible to describe and analyse other sets of historical events. Such people have argued that the Holocaust can be apprehended at best only partially, through the individual memories of survivors or through artistic representations [94]. In works of these types greater emphasis is often placed upon evoking strong emotions than upon conveying strict factual precision; frequently they produce a feeling of shock, mystery, and bewilderment over how the horrors that characterized the encounter could ever have taken place.

The chapters that follow, while not negating this manner of dealing with the subject, take a different approach. They try to offer first of all a dispassionate look at the basic facts of the encounter between the Third Reich and the Jews – the who-what-when-where-how of the case. Then they attempt to place those facts in a historical context, reconstructing the thoughts of participants in the encounter, Germans and Jews alike, in a way that, it is hoped, will allow bewilderment to yield to a sense that events unfolded as they did for intelligible reasons. They appeal, in other words, not to readers' emotions but to their intellects; they demand of them a mental effort to enter into the minds of people whose way of looking at the world was very different from their own, and at times even altogether alien to it. In the end, readers will decide for themselves to what degree their efforts and the book's have rendered the Holocaust comprehensible.

2   THE JEWS

The leaders of the Third Reich defined millions of Jews out of humanity. They viewed all Jews as their mortal enemies and on that basis justified their systematic mass killing, no matter what any individual Jew
said, did, or believed.

Who were these Jews who so bedevilled and frightened them?

JEWISH ORIGINS

The word 'Jew' is derived from the name Judah, who was one of the
sons of the Biblical patriarch Jacob. Judah (or in its Greek variant,
Judea) was also the name of a political entity that existed in the eastern
Mediterranean region from at least a thousand years before the birth
of Jesus to more than a century thereafter. At times Judea was a fully
independent country; at other times it was a province of a foreign
empire (Babylonian, Persian, Greek, or Roman). Its boundaries varied,
but its centre was in the hill country south of Jerusalem between the
Mediterranean coast and the Jordan River. Originally the word 'Jew'
was used to designate what might be called today a citizen of Judea –
someone whose right to reside in that country was inalienable and
could be passed on from generation to generation. It was, in other
words, primarily a political term.

Already in ancient times, though, the name was employed in other
senses as well. As early as the sixth century BCE Jews had settled outside Judea, and by Hellenistic times they had established communities
throughout much of the eastern Mediterranean area. These Judean
emigrants and their descendants continued often to be referred to as
Jews, on the grounds that initially they or their ancestors had come
from Judea; their communities came to be referred to collectively as a
'diaspora' – a word of Greek origin meaning 'scattering'. In this way,
the word 'Jew' was used as what might be called an ethnic designa-
tion. Such usage was facilitated by the fact that Jews in the diaspora

generally continued to observe a set of laws that they believed their God had revealed to their ancestors long ago and that were binding upon Jews alone. Their continued observance of these laws in addition to local laws set them off as a distinct group among the peoples in whose midst they lived. Thus the term 'Jew' acquired religious as well as political and ethnic associations.

In the ancient world it was not unusual for states, provinces, or ethnic groups to have their own particular religions. Religion and ethnicity, in other words, were not easily separated in ancient times. During the Hellenistic era, however, a tendency emerged among members of various ethnic groups to develop a common religious core that transcended ethnic origins. This movement was reinforced with the appearance of Christianity, which claimed the status of a universal religion, one that all people could accept and practice no matter to which group or country they belonged. Jews, however, remained by and large an exception to this trend. The polytheistic peoples of the ancient world were amenable to religious syncretism largely because each people perceived fundamental similarities between its gods and those of its neighbours. In contrast, most Jews believed that their God was the sole omnipotent lord of the entire universe, who demanded that the Jewish people serve that God and that God alone; hence they could not join other peoples in any religious endeavour that would require them to acknowledge the reality of other gods or to compromise the manner in which they carried out their God-given law. Although some Jews disagreed with this approach, an internal struggle in the middle of the second century BCE effectively put an end to open syncretistic tendencies among them.

This refusal to be merged into a universal religion often made Jews an object of intense curiosity in the ancient world. Sometimes it even led to violent clashes between Jews and their neighbours. But it also helped them to preserve their identity as a distinct people after the Romans eliminated Judea as a political entity in the year 135.

THE JEWS IN CHRISTIAN EUROPE

Jews established diaspora communities in Mediterranean Europe already in pre-Christian times, but not until the tenth century are Jews known to have established permanent settlements north of the Alps. The most important of these early communities were located in German-speaking regions, mainly in the Rhein valley. Jews referred to these regions by the Hebrew name Ashkenaz; Jews who lived there came to be known as Ashkenazic Jews, to distinguish them from Jews in the Mediterranean countries and the Middle East, who were called Sefardic Jews. In the early Middle Ages Sefardic Jews were far more numerous, but over the centuries Ashkenazic Jews increased in number, until by the early twentieth century they made up almost 90 per cent of world Jewry. Although in ancient times Jews were largely an agricultural people, the Ashkenazic communities were based mainly on commerce. Initially European rulers welcomed the Jews' contribution to their economies; in the highly localized feudal system, in which most of the population worked the land, Jews (along with other foreign minorities) played a vital role in promoting exchange among far-flung territories, especially between Christian Europe and the Islamic world. To encourage them in this endeavour, rulers, in accordance with the common medieval practice of decentralizing political authority, granted Jews special charters of rights that allowed them to establish their own autonomous institutions and live according to their own laws. However, by the twelfth century a growing native Christian merchant class came into conflict with the Jews. This clash contributed to a concomitant spread throughout Europe of stereotypes portraying Jews as a serious danger to Christian society; indeed, many historians have pointed to the twelfth and thirteenth centuries as a time when European society was especially intolerant not only of Jews but of minorities in general [73; 98; 131]. Another expression of popular hostility towards Jews during this period came in the form of repeated attacks upon Ashkenazic communities that accompanied the Crusades. In the wake of these attacks many Jews migrated from the Germanic lands to Poland, where conditions resembled those of the earlier Middle Ages farther west. By the sixteenth century Poland became a major centre of Ashkenazic Jewry.

Contrary to a common misperception, the medieval Church leadership generally did not encourage violence against Jews. Officially its position was that Jews must be allowed to live among Christians, although their status must be visibly degraded in order to remind Christians of the dire consequences of denying the divinity of Jesus. In accordance with this principle, Church leaders protested at times against the relatively beneficent treatment Jews often received from secular rulers who valued their commercial services. They demanded that Jews wear special types of clothing to mark them as different, and they called for measures to segregate them from Christian society as much as possible. But they also tried to restrain the common people who, under the influence of hostile stereotypes, lashed out physically every so often against their Jewish neighbours, and they opposed efforts to convert Jews by force. Still, the extent to which

Church teachings, especially as transmitted to the common people by various segments of the Church hierarchy, helped to foment an ongoing climate of violent hostility towards Jews in Christian Europe remains a matter of controversy among scholars [72; 169; 179].

Church requirements that Jews be visibly marked off from Christians were not always enforced. Nonetheless, Jews were often easily distinguishable from Christians by their dress and grooming customs, dietary habits, educational practices, and social networks, as well as by their heavy involvement in commerce and virtual absence from agriculture and artisanry. Jewish religious law, especially prohibitions on consuming certain foods and beverages, helped reinforce social separation. Moreover, in many Ashkenazic communities Jews spoke their own distinct language, called Yiddish. This language was based upon the Germanic dialect spoken in the Rhein valley when Jews first settled there, with vocabulary added from Hebrew, the Slavic languages, Latin, and old French. For written communication Ashkenazic Jews employed mainly Hebrew; gradually they developed a written form of Yiddish as well, using the Hebrew alphabet.

As popular and clerical pressure against Jews mounted, secular rulers often concluded that the Jewish communities in their territories were more a liability than an asset. King Edward I of England expelled all Jews from his realm in 1290. Expulsions from most French territories followed during the fourteenth century, from Spain in 1492, and from many of the German states during the next two hundred years. In other places, beginning in sixteenth-century Italy and later in central Europe, Jews were confined to closed neighbourhoods, often called ghettos*. In general, the later Middle Ages were a period in which European Jewish existence was less secure than it had been in earlier centuries. Nevertheless, in most places where Jews lived they enjoyed considerable autonomy, governing themselves largely according to their own laws.

IN MODERN TIMES

The precariousness of the Jewish situation began to recede in the late seventeenth century. The appearance of capitalism with its emphasis upon individual freedom and initiative, the spread of rational philosophy and the notion of religious tolerance, the emergence of centralized state administrations in place of the medieval system of corporate estates – all of these led various elements of European society to rethink their attitudes towards Jews. Some began to argue that if states treated them on the same basis as all other subjects, Jews would become productive and loyal members of the larger society. Such thinking was evident in Oliver Cromwell's effective suspension of the ban upon Jewish settlement in England during the 1650s. However, others maintained that the non-universalistic nature of the Jewish religion prevented Jews from identifying with the peoples among whom they lived. They claimed that Jews would always be a distinct people, more concerned with the welfare of their fellow Jews in faraway lands than with that of their closest non-Jewish neighbours.

In the late eighteenth and early nineteenth centuries, several European countries decided to test which view was correct. In 1782 Emperor Joseph II of Austria issued an Edict of Toleration, which removed many medieval restrictions upon Jewish residence and economic activity [22]. It was widely understood, though, that in return Jews were expected to dress and groom themselves like their neighbours, speak the language of the country, educate their children according to the demands of the state, expand their range of occupations, and renounce all claims to autonomy or special group status. Revolutionary France granted Jews civic equality on similar terms, as did many of the countries that fell under French influence as a result of Napoleon's conquests. By 1871, Jews had been 'emancipated' – made equal citizens – in all of the European states west of the Elbe River, with the expectation that they view themselves as Frenchmen, Germans, or Englishmen of the Jewish religion instead of as members of a single historic people scattered throughout the world. Most Jews in these countries welcomed this bargain; they declared that the term 'Jew' now referred to a religious group only and no longer had any ethnic significance. They worked hard to eliminate the economic, social, linguistic, and cultural distinctions that had visibly separated them from their surrounding societies in medieval times. Some, known as Reform Jews, even proposed far-reaching changes in Jewish religious law, including elimination of dietary prohibitions, in order to facilitate social integration. By the end of the nineteenth century, most western European Jews had done much to make themselves superficially indistinguishable from their neighbours in many respects, speaking the same language, attending the same schools, reading the same books and newspapers, wearing the same clothes. And as the economies of their countries prospered, they prospered too.

These developments, however, affected only a minority of Europe's Jews. The majority, more than 5 million in 1880, lived in the Russian Empire, which had taken over most of Poland between 1772 and 1815. Tsarist Russia did not offer Jews civic equality; hence a major impulse towards integration was absent among Russo-Polish Jewry.

Moreover, the country's relative economic underdevelopment kept the bulk of its Jews in poverty. Most of these Jews continued into the twentieth century to be distinguished from the surrounding society in language, culture, social organization, and occupational structure as well as in religion. Many eastern European Jews, influenced by ideas of nationalism, began to define themselves as members of a Jewish nation and to demand national rights. Zionism*, which emerged during the 1880s, claimed that Jews had a right to establish their own nation-state in the historic Jewish homeland. Other Jewish nationalist movements sought autonomy for Jews within multicultural European bourgeois or socialist states.

From the late 1870s through to 1914, almost 3 million eastern European Jews, seeking better economic and political conditions, migrated westward, increasing the Jewish populations of Germany, France, and England and turning the United States, with 4.4 million Jews in 1930, into the world's largest Jewish community. Especially in Germany, the influx of these foreign Jews helped strengthen the hand of those who opposed Jewish civic equality. During the 1880s these German opponents formed political parties and pressure groups with the goal of curtailing Jewish rights; calling themselves 'antisemites', they demanded that Jews be removed from the civil service and free professions, denied citizenship, taxed discriminatorily, and forbidden from migrating to Germany. Similar groups emerged in other European countries. Yet although they attracted much attention, nowhere did they achieve their legislative goals. In Germany they were an insignificant political force before the First World War [118; 136].

With the overthrow of the tsarist regime in 1917 and the establishment of new states after the First World War, the Jewish masses of eastern Europe gained formal civic equality. However, their strong Jewish national identity often clashed with the equally strong nationalist feelings of the Poles, Lithuanians, Romanians, and other eastern European peoples who had acquired state power. Such clashes impeded social integration and the redefinition of Jews as a religious group along western European lines. Particularly in Poland, which regained independence in 1918 and became home to Europe's largest Jewish population (3.3 million in 1931), Jews retained many attributes of a distinct national group: they spoke mainly Yiddish (although their use of Polish increased steadily); maintained their own schools, theatres, health and welfare organizations, and political parties; published their own daily newspapers; and lived in compact Jewish neighbourhoods. Many Poles looked upon Jews as alien competitors for jobs and hoped to see their country's Jewish population substantially reduced through emigration. The same was true in other eastern European countries with large Jewish populations – particularly Romania, with 750,000 Jews in 1930, and Hungary, with 450,000 [145]. The 3 million Jews of the Soviet Union were subjected to intense governmental pressure to merge into that country's socialist economy and society. As a result, integration proceeded more rapidly there than elsewhere in eastern Europe, but the size of the Jewish community and its nationalist heritage helped many Soviet Jews preserve a measure of cultural uniqueness. Also, although only a relatively small number of Jews were attracted to communism, Jews had been prominent among the leaders of the Bolshevik revolution. Hence Jews were often identified invidiously with Bolshevism by the eastern European peoples who had fallen under Soviet domination or who feared the spread of communism into their own countries [186].

A reasonable assessment of the Jewish situation in Europe around 1930 would thus have placed Germany's 525,000 Jews among the continent's most secure. Representing less than 1 per cent of the country's population, German Jews were on the whole economically well off; their civic equality, which appeared untouchable, had allowed them to become prominent in German cultural, economic, and political life. Socially they were gaining acceptance as well; by the 1920s one of every four German Jews was marrying into a non-Jewish family. In fact, some German Jewish leaders saw intermarriage as a much greater threat to their community's survival than the hostility of the surrounding society, which appeared far milder and less extensive than in eastern Europe [155]. That a German government would shortly seek to kill not only all German Jews but millions of Jews beyond the country's borders was not a possibility that any Jewish leader anywhere in the world entertained [119].

PART TWO: ANALYSIS

3 HITLER, NAZIS, GERMANS, AND JEWS

The German government that undertook the systematic mass killing of Europe's Jews was dominated by the National Socialist German Workers (Nazi) Party*, led by Adolf Hitler. Historians of Germany continue to debate whether the Third Reich is best understood as Hitler's personal creation, as a product of programmes generated out of the broader ideas and goals of the Nazi party, or as the outcome of historical developments, within Germany or beyond, whose origins predate the Nazi period. The same questions animate academic discussions about the origins of the Holocaust. In 1996 Daniel Goldhagen aroused great controversy among scholars with his statement that the idea of killing Jews had been 'immanent in the conversation of German society' for over a century [100 *p. 449*]. To his mind, Hitler and the Nazi party were not central to the development among the German people of the notion that Jews were dangerous enemies who deserved to die; that notion, he claimed, was an integral part of modern German culture.

Most historians have rejected Goldhagen's thesis. Many have pointed out that the major features of what Goldhagen termed 'eliminationist antisemitism', which he argued was a uniquely German idea that predated the rise of Nazism, were in fact present among other European peoples in the nineteenth and twentieth centuries no less than among the Germans; but in the absence of Nazi-like leadership they did not lead to systematic mass murder [48; 56; 62]. Hence the question of how a *German* government, and not that of another people, came during the 1930s and 1940s to launch what Lucy Dawidowicz called a 'war against the Jews' [77], on the pretext that Jews were non-human pathogens who threatened human survival, continues to perplex scholars and non-scholars alike.

THE JEWS IN HITLER'S WORLD-VIEW

One thing is certain: Hitler himself repeatedly expressed the view that Jews represented a deadly menace to all people on earth. In one of his earliest recorded political speeches, on 13 August 1920 [*Doc. 2*], he called Jews 'parasites,' claiming that 'from early on [the Jew] felt the need to rule over the peoples among whom he lived, which meant first of all to destroy the inner fabric of their countries' [23 *pp. 409, 411*]. And in his final political testament, dictated on 29 April 1945, the day before he died, he called upon the Germans to continue 'to fight mercilessly against the poisoners of all the peoples of the world, international Jewry' [2 *p. 162*].

This perception was not simply the result of blind hatred, nor was it merely an unthinking repetition of medieval or modern anti-Jewish calumnies (although many historians assert that 'the Nazis did not add any new elements to antisemitism' [52 *p. 89*]). Rather it was a conclusion derived from a complex (though preposterous) general world-view [116]. In his autobiographical work, *Mein Kampf**, written in 1924–26, as well as in an untitled, unpublished second book written in 1928, Hitler hinted at how his view of Jews flowed logically, to his mind, from more fundamental ideas about the nature of human beings and human history.

Indeed, in retrospect that view seems clearly to have been rooted in Hitler's central conviction that 'all occurrences in world history are only the expression of the races' instinct of self-preservation, in the good or bad sense' [14 *p. 296*]. This statement indicated first of all that, like many people in his time, Hitler divided humanity into distinct biological groups, each supposedly displaying a unique, genetically derived essence or spirit. Following common usage of the day, he often termed these groups 'races' – a word that suggested less skin colour than a gene pool. Sometimes he used the words 'peoples' (*Völker**) or 'nations' to describe them as well. The behaviour of individual members of these 'races' or 'peoples', according to Hitler, could be understood as manifestations of shared hereditary tendencies; people acted as they did because they were genetically ('racially') inclined to do so. Hence, Hitler deduced, if individuals appear to demonstrate an inborn will to live, then the various races to which they belong must also naturally possess a collective instinct for self-preservation.

Hitler claimed that this collective instinct could be observed, as in individuals, in two fundamental human drives – for food and for reproduction. Each race, to his mind, naturally sought to maximize both its food supply and the number of its offspring. To accomplish these goals, he reasoned, each race required land, where it could grow food and raise progeny. However, as he observed in his second book, although 'the population grows incessantly, ... the soil as such remains stationary' [15 *p. 15*], meaning that the more successful a race was in producing offspring, the greater the difficulty it faced in feeding them. The only way for a race to escape this dilemma, according to Hitler, was constantly to increase the amount of land at its disposal; yet by doing so it would inevitably clash with other races seeking to do the same thing, because the total amount of land in the world was finite. Each race's attempt to satisfy its instinct of self-preservation, in other words, had, to Hitler's mind, necessarily to lead it into conflict with all other races. Hitler regarded this eternal conflict as the basic motive force in human history; hence 'all occurrences in world history are only the expression of the races' instinct of self-preservation'.

Jews presented an obvious problem for this theory. Hitler identified them initially as a race, not a religious community. According to his central conviction, this racial status ought to have made them struggle for land throughout their history. But in fact Jews had controlled no territory of their own for many centuries. If Hitler's view of human history was correct, this lack of territory should have caused the Jews to disappear many years before. Yet instead of concluding that his theory was flawed, Hitler decided that Jews must have found a secret way to survive without land. In the culminating passage of his second book he observed that 'as a support of its own existence [the Jewish people] needs the work and creative activities of other nations'. An organism that cannot survive on its own but must attach itself to another organism in order to ensure its food supply is a parasite; hence Hitler concluded that 'the existence of the Jew himself becomes a parasitical one within the lives of other peoples' [15 *p. 212*].

Others had portrayed Jews as parasites before, but none seems to have taken the analogy nearly as literally as Hitler did. During his youth in Vienna Hitler had been influenced by occult racist circles that – all sense data to the contrary – posited the existence of non-human creatures with human bodies and called them an evil principle that destroyed life itself [101; 151]. Hitler's theory of history allowed him to infer that Jews were in fact such creatures. Because the way in which they struggled for survival was fundamentally different from that of all other peoples, he reasoned, they could not be a true human race; rather 'their apparently great sense of solidarity is based on the very primitive herd instinct' of animals [14 *p. 301*]. They could survive, he concluded, only through a planned, coordinated effort to weaken all genuinely human peoples; they were genetically compelled to insinuate themselves slowly into other societies, mating with non-Jewish young women in order 'to destroy the racial foundations of the people [they] have set out to subjugate'. 'Just as [the Jew] systematically ruins women and girls', he wrote, 'he does not shrink back from pulling down the blood barriers for others, even on a large scale. It ... is Jews who bring the Negroes into the Rhineland, always with the same secret thought ... of ruining the hated white race by the necessarily resulting bastardization, throwing it down from its cultural and political height, and ... rising to be its master' [14 *p. 325*]. Ultimately, he declared, 'wherever [the Jew] appears, the host people dies out' [14 *p. 305*].

It follows from such a literal conception of the Jew as noxious parasite that Jews were mortal enemies not of Germany alone but of all humanity; indeed, Hitler stated clearly that 'if ... the Jew is victorious over the other peoples of the world, his crown will be the funeral wreath of humanity and this planet will ... move through the ether devoid of men'. This belief, in turn, gave Hitler's proposed struggle against the Jews a messianic quality: 'I believe that ... *by defending myself against the Jew, I am fighting for the work of the Lord*' [14 *p. 65*]. Historian Saul Friedländer has called this 'distinctive aspect of [Hitler's] world view "redemptive anti-Semitism"' and concluded that 'it was this redemptive dimension ... that led to Hitler's ultimate decision that the Jews were to be exterminated' [92 *p. 3*].

JEWS IN THE IDEOLOGY AND PROGRAMME OF NAZISM

Other historians, though aware of Hitler's thoughts about the Jews, question whether they are the most important facts to note in explaining the German war against the Jews. After all, a single individual could not have launched such a war unless his proposed anti-Jewish struggle made sense to many others in his country. Hence they have asked who those other Germans were and how they came to the conclusion that Jews everywhere ought to be killed.

One of the earliest attempts to explain the systematic mass killing of Jews claimed that such killing was an essential consequence of a broader German ideology called national socialism or Nazism, which the Nazi party was organized to implement and spread. Nazism, according to this view, taught 'that all traditional doctrines and values must be rejected ..., whether liberal or absolutist, democratic or socialist', in order to establish Germany as the world's foremost power [153 *p. 38*]. National socialists justified their demand for world domination by claiming that Germans constituted a genetically ('racially') superior people whose biological supremacy entitled them to political pre-eminence. No existing political doctrine, whether of the right or the left, recognized the possibility that such a claim could ever be valid; hence, it was asserted, national socialists were compelled to eliminate those doctrines altogether, along with anyone who persisted in espousing them. To those who viewed national socialism in this way, Jews appeared to be the first people slated for elimination, both because they were convenient symbols of such non-racially based ideas as liberalism, socialism, and Christianity, and because their social situation suited them uniquely to serve as 'guinea pigs for testing the method of repression'. According to this perception of Nazi ideology and practice, however, 'not only Jews [were bound to] fall under the executioner's ax but ... countless others of many races, nationalities, beliefs, and religions ...; the extermination of the Jews [was] only the means to the attainment of the ultimate objective, namely the destruction of free institutions, beliefs, and groups' [153 *pp. 550–1*]. In other words, national socialism demonstrated murderous potential towards a variety of enemies; it felt no special enmity towards Jews *per se*.

The author of this interpretation, Franz Neumann, himself a Jewish refugee from the Nazi regime, did not attribute these national socialist ideas to Hitler; in fact, he did not ascribe them initially to any specific individuals or groups. In his opinion, 'the ideologies [that national socialism] uses or discards are mere ... techniques of domination' [153 *p. 467*]. Persecution of Jews, he suggested, had a long history in Germany and elsewhere, and it was strongly rooted in popular anti-Jewish stereotypes and prejudices; thus it could easily be employed to unify the German people against 'one enemy who can easily be exterminated and who cannot resist' [153 *p. 125*]. From this premise it followed that the roots of the Holocaust were not to be found in any new idea or world-view – Hitler's own thoughts notwithstanding – but simply in the desire of national socialists to consolidate their rule: Jews were persecuted, and eventually killed, because it made good political sense to do so.

The theme that the war against the Jews was designed to facilitate the broader nihilistic war against all of Western civilization preached by national socialists had been sounded even before the onset of mass killing by Hermann Rauschning, a Nazi senator from Danzig who quit the party in 1934 [*Doc. 3*]. Variations of it were put forth by several important scholars during the first three decades following the Nazi defeat [57; 150; 158]. Studies of what Nazis other than Hitler thought about Jews seemed to strengthen this conclusion: relatively few appear to have joined the party primarily in order to strike against the

Jewish enemy as conceived by Hitler. Nazis who later played key roles in the killing of Jews, including Heinrich Himmler*, Hermann Goering*, Hans Frank*, and Adolf Eichmann*, evidently acquired their radical animus towards Jews after becoming Nazis, not before [34; 102; 146].

However, other historians have noted several facts that this view does not easily explain. For example, the question has been raised why it was necessary for the Third Reich not merely to *persecute* Jews but to kill them. The enormous distance between persecution and murder was revealed dramatically at a meeting between Hitler and his ally, the Hungarian regent Miklos Horthy*, on 17 April 1943. Discussing how to control the social damage Jews were allegedly causing in his country, Horthy asked what he ought to do about them. The Hungarian leader explained that he had already moved to destroy the Jews economically; the only remaining measure that could be taken against them was to kill them, but that, as far as he was concerned, was unthinkable [*Doc. 4*]. In other words, the Hungarian ruler could oppress Jews with little compunction, but he could not conceive of murdering them *en masse*. A mental gulf appears to have separated him from the leaders of the Third Reich, who had already accomplished the leap from persecution to total, systematic murder. Enslaving the Jews – including selective killing of Jewish leaders, the destruction of Jewish social and cultural institutions, and the elimination of the basis of their economic life (what Raphael Lemkin called 'genocide') – ought to have accomplished the instrumental goals that Neumann, Rauschning, and others ascribed to the anti-Jewish aspect of national socialism. Indeed, Neumann had predicted in 1942 that 'the internal political value of Anti-Semitism will ... never allow a complete extermination of the Jews', because 'the foe ... must always be held in readiness as a scapegoat for all the evils originating in the socio-political system' [153 *p. 125*]. Systematic total killing did not unambiguously advance those goals. Why, then, did it take place?

Nor is it clear that the leaders of the Third Reich ever had serious plans to visit the fate of the Jews upon a broad range of other groups. To be sure, the thought was raised from time to time that Poles and other Slavic peoples ought to disappear from the face of the earth; Hans Frank, head of the part of occupied Poland called the General-gouvernement*, even declared that 'once we have won the war, for my part all the Poles and Ukrainians and the rest that are roaming around here can be made into mincemeat' [180 *p. 39*]. However, Third Reich policy-makers seem to have been reluctant to act on such ideas. Erhard Wetzel, head of the Department of Racial Policy in the

Ministry of the Occupied Eastern Territories, explained that 'it should be obvious that the Polish question cannot be solved by liquidating the Poles as we are doing with the Jews', as 'such a solution of the Polish question would weigh upon the German people into the distant future ... and cause our neighbours to figure that at some point they will be treated the same way' [7 *p. 308*].

And Hans Frank noted in his diary on 14 December 1942 that it would be impossible to kill even all those Poles who were unfit for labour service, because 'the extirpation of millions of human beings depends upon certain preconditions that at present we cannot fulfill' [30, 29 *p. 565*].

When Frank wrote those words, more than 2 million Jews had already been murdered by the Third Reich. Evidently he thought about Poles and Jews not as similar obstacles to the goals of national socialism but in fundamentally different terms: Poles were human beings, Jews were not. Hence, whereas Nazi officials could ask whether mass murder of Poles would be an effective means to the Third Reich's basic ends, it does not seem to have occurred to them to ask the same question regarding Jews. Wetzel's apprehensions about how Germany's good name would be affected and how other peoples might react to the killing of Poles were not at issue in the case of the Jews. Murder of Jews thus appears to have been considered more as an end in itself than as a means to some other goal; it was an action that the Third Reich felt compelled to take no matter what the immediate consequences. It could not, then, have been simply a by-product of national socialism.

JEWS IN GERMAN PUBLIC OPINION

Similarly, the idea that the mass killing of Jews helped the Nazi party solidify its standing among the German people assumes that most Germans supported the killing. However, studies of German public responses to Nazi anti-Jewish practices at various stages in the history of the Third Reich have shown that those practices did not always enhance the party's popularity and often were more extreme than mainstream popular opinion found acceptable. In 1929–33, when the Nazis were competing successfully in democratic elections, their propaganda usually did not stress how they proposed to deal with Jews; party spokesmen tended to refer to the Jewish theme only in abstract terms, toning down anti-Jewish rhetoric, integrating it into the discussion of broader political and economic concerns, and obscuring specific plans for anti-Jewish action [68; 107]. Hence in his work on the Nazi rise to power in Bavaria, Geoffrey Pridham concluded that 'the majority of voters did not ... realize how seriously the Nazis meant to put their [anti-Jewish] ideas into practice ...' [163 *p. 244*]. The promise of specific measures to be taken against Jews does not appear to have been a strong drawing card for the Nazis at the polls [102]. Indeed, W.S. Allen's study of a small town in Hannover found that 'many who voted Nazi simply ignored or rationalized the anti-semitism of the party, just as they ignored other unpleasant aspects of the Nazi movement'. In his famous formulation, the townspeople 'were drawn to anti-semitism because they were drawn to Nazism, not the other way around' [37 *p. 77*].

After the Nazi party came to power in 1933, it found a public highly ambivalent about how the regime ought to relate to Jews. Although feeling seems to have prevailed among Germans that their Jewish neighbours exercised excessive influence in the administration of their country and in its cultural and economic life, few evidently regarded that situation as one of Germany's most serious problems [42; 122]. Hence even some opponents of the regime initially accepted discriminatory laws aimed at reducing that influence, like the April 1933 dismissal of Jews from the civil service; and many more were indifferent, preferring not to trouble themselves with the Jews' legal status [42; 92]. Similarly, the 1935 Nuremberg Laws*, which effectively revoked Jews' German citizenship and outlawed marriages between Jews and non-Jews, met with widespread public acquiescence [42; 124; 129]. On the other hand, considerable public dissatisfaction was recorded whenever the regime engaged in anti-Jewish violence. In particular, the so-called Kristallnacht* riots of November 1938, with their countrywide looting of Jewish shops and homes and burning of Jewish public institutions, aroused revulsion among significant segments of the German populace – although many Germans seem to have been bothered more by the pogrom's disorder and wanton brutality than by any sense of obligation towards their Jewish countrymen [42; 102; 129]. Brutal physical attacks upon Jewish life, limb, and property thus might not have called forth vigorous public protest against the regime, but they were hardly an effective way to mobilize public support. Indeed, when the regime finally embarked upon its programme of systematic mass killing in 1941, it took pains to keep information about the murders from the public, evidently convinced that 'it could not rely on popular backing for its extermination policy' [124 *p. 289*; 132].

Hence many historians have rejected the notion that the Holocaust can be satisfactorily explained as an essential product either of national socialism or of widespread popular German hostility towards

Jews. Instead they have directed their attention to the processes that might have made at least a minimum critical mass of Germans receptive to the idea that Jews were noxious parasites who needed to be killed. Some have examined a relatively small circle of 'true believers' in Hitler's world-view – estimated by Saul Friedländer at about 10 per cent of the adult German population – in order to explore 'the formation ... of a collective consciousness governed by total inversion of the most widely accepted human moral values' [90 *p. 146*].

TRUE BELIEVERS AND THE FIRST WORLD WAR

One detailed study of Nazi party members before 1933 showed slightly over half seriously believing that Jews represented in some way a significant threat to Germany. Of these, almost 60 per cent suggested that Germany's defeat in the First World War and the political revolution that followed had shocked them into this conviction [146]. The finding was not surprising, for the aftermath of the defeat had witnessed a sharp upsurge in German expressions of anti-Jewish antipathy. That upsurge could be explained by recalling the strange circumstances in which Germans learned that their country had lost the war: no foreign troops had yet set foot on German soil, and German soldiers continued to occupy large sections of enemy territory. Thus many Germans concluded that they had won the war on the battlefield, only to be 'stabbed in the back' by enemies within. Some were inclined to identify those internal enemies as Jews. During the war, Jews as a group had been accused of shirking military service and of profiteering, and Jews had been prominent among those calling for an end to the fighting through a negotiated peace. When, in the days following the imperial German collapse, radical socialists, including the Jews Kurt Eisner and Rosa Luxemburg, threatened to establish a new government based upon workers' and soldiers' councils, many recalled the association of Jews with Bolshevism, concluding that Jews wished to enslave Germany to the communist yoke. The postwar Weimar Republic*, regarded by many Germans as an Allied imposition against the will of the German people, featured many Jews among its architects, so it was not long before opponents branded it the 'Jew-Republic' [157]. In this context, a line portraying Jews as potential destroyers of Germany found readier acceptance among Germans than it had in less troubled times.

In *Mein Kampf*, Hitler played heavily upon the associations between Jews and the German defeat, Bolshevism, and the Weimar Republic. He presented Marxism and Bolshevism as the Jews' main weapons in their perverted struggle for survival: by preaching international working-class solidarity across racial lines, these doctrines deflected people's loyalties from their own racial groups, thereby weakening each nation's ability to mobilize its members in the constant battle for land. Hence, he explained, 'for every hero who had volunteered and mounted the steps of Valhalla after a heroic death ..., there was a slacker who had cautiously turned his back on death' in order to establish the Weimar regime [14 *p. 521*]. Such slackers were, to his mind, 'Marxist gangsters', while 'the *real* organizer of the revolution and its actual wirepuller' was 'the international Jew' [14 *pp. 522–3*]. Thus he reasoned that 'in exact proportion as, in the course of the War, the German worker and the German soldier fell ... into the hands of the Marxist leaders, in exactly that proportion he was lost to the fatherland'; and he concluded that 'if at the beginning of the War and during the War twelve or fifteen thousand of these Hebrew corrupters of the people had been held under poison gas ..., the sacrifice of millions at the front would not have been in vain' [14 *p. 679*]. To be sure, Hitler was not the only German to express such ideas; after the war a number of groups organized to combat the alleged Jewish-Marxist conspiracy that had created the Weimar Republic [152; 157]. Yet Hitler's analysis may have been especially credible to some because it was rooted in a comprehensive, seemingly scientific world-view – one that could show not only *that* Jews were dangerous but *why* they were so and suggest effective action for removing the danger.

Still, that analysis appears to have made sense at first to only a few Germans. Before 1930, the Nazi party never received more than 6.6 per cent of the vote in any parliamentary election, and evidently most Nazi votes were not cast mainly because of Hitler's ideas about Jews. Some scholars have thus asked whether Hitler's true believers shared any special characteristics that made them respond to the First World War and its aftermath precisely as they did and differently from other Germans. Efforts to answer this question have centred on constructing a common social or psychological profile of the group; but aside from the generalization that members of the middle class, broadly defined, were more receptive to Hitler's message about the Jews than members of other social strata, such a profile has proven elusive [90; 102; 137]. Moreover, even if a clear profile could be established, it would not explain how over time the number of Germans prepared to play a role in the systematic mass killing of Jews came to extend beyond this limited circle. Indeed, as the researches of Raul Hilberg and Christopher Browning [63; 64; 112], among others, have shown, the Holocaust could not have happened without the participation of many other Germans – soldiers, civil servants, doctors, lawyers, industrialists, clerks, railway workers, even clergymen – who were not ideologically committed Nazis of long standing yet who helped locate Jews, identify them, imprison them, and kill them without protest or attempts at evasion. If, as studies of German public opinion have suggested, most Germans did not display especially violent inclinations towards Jews even after the Nazi regime came to power, where did these participants in the killing process come from?

ORDINARY MEN OR ORDINARY GERMANS?

Aside from Goldhagen and a handful of others [165; 190] who continue to posit a unique German national character, arising out of the peculiarities of German history since the Reformation, which – public opinion studies notwithstanding – ostensibly made the German people as a whole especially receptive to the notion that Jews were their mortal enemies, attempts to answer this question have taken two approaches. One has stressed general psychological factors – careerism, peer pressure, deference to authority – that under the brutalizing influences of modern warfare might have turned virtually anyone into a killer. As Browning, who studied a German reserve police battalion involved in killing operations in Poland, noted:

> there are many societies afflicted by ... racism and caught in the siege mentality of war. ... Everywhere society conditions people to respect ... authority. ... Everywhere people seek career advancement. In every modern society ... bureaucratization and specialization attenuate the sense of personal responsibility of those implementing official policy. Within ... every social collective, the peer group ... sets moral norms. If the men of Reserve Police Battalion 101 could become killers under such circumstances, what group of men cannot? [64 *pp. 188–9*].

In this view the perpetrators and facilitators of the Holocaust were ultimately 'ordinary men' (indeed, there were few women among them), and their behaviour was but marginally influenced by a specific ideological conception of Jews.

The other approach has accorded more weight to ideology, suggesting that the specific Nazi environment in which they lived was ultimately decisive in eroding the perpetrators' natural human aversion to killing. A proponent of this view has argued that appeals to universal behavioural patterns have inadequately considered 'the broader background, the larger contextual and mental structures that *shaped the choices made,* guided action and created the atmosphere in which decisions proceeded and the [killing] machine operated' [40 *p. 144*].

Killers, in other words, were less 'ordinary men' than 'ordinary Germans' – not, in Goldhagen's sense, as bearers of a longstanding German cultural tradition but as people gradually imbued after 1933 with the basic values of *Nazi* Germany. Scholars inclined to this position have thus emphasized the importance of indoctrination, exploring the social and educational channels – the Hitler Youth*, the Reich Labour Service*, and the Army, among others – through which Nazi leaders and true believers might have persuaded ever greater numbers of Germans that Jews everywhere deserved to die [47; 97].

The best answer probably lies somewhere between these poles, in 'a combination of ideological and situational factors that allowed a popular, ideologically driven, dictatorial regime and its hardcore followers to mobilize and harness the rest of society to its purposes', including the systematic mass murder of Jews [62 *p. 108*]. Clearly, the Holocaust was born in the first instance out of the interaction of a German leadership viewing Jews as noxious parasites with a German public potentially animated by motives rooted both in universal psychology and in the German historical, social, and cultural environment. The nature of that interaction and the relative weight of the motives, however, remain matters for debate.

4   1933–41 – A TWISTED ROAD?

The controversy over whether the participation of Germans other than long-standing Nazi true believers is best explained through deliberate indoctrination or universal human psychology is only part of a broader historiographical discussion. That discussion asks whether Nazism as a whole should be represented as a unique incursion of evil into history or as a phenomenon that, no matter how horrible, grew out of normal historical processes and human behaviours. In the mid-1980s German historian Martin Broszat issued a 'plea for the historicization of national socialism', by which he appears to have meant that historians should not presuppose that the Third Reich took decisions and formulated policies any differently from other modern governments, whatever their ideological orientations. Broszat charged that scholars of the Third Reich often explained Nazi actions in terms that they would not employ for other regimes, because they were more concerned with condemning Nazi atrocities than with understanding them. Thus, he held, they were unable to see Nazi leaders as anything but criminals. Broszat did not deny or make light of Nazi criminality, but he suggested that Nazis did not set out from the beginning to do evil for evil's sake [67].

Broszat's position was widely criticized. Saul Friedländer, while agreeing that 'during the Nazi era, few domains – with the exception of direct criminal activities – can be considered as entirely abhorrent', insisted nevertheless that 'very few domains can be considered as entirely untouched by some of the ... criminal aspects of the core' [91 p. 73]. Because of the Third Reich's 'criminal core', he argued, 'writing about Nazism [cannot be] like writing about sixteenth-century France' [91 p. 80]. In explaining the behaviour of 'ordinary' participants in the killing process, then, historians who stress the importance of ideological indoctrination might be applying Friedländer's approach. Universal psychological explanations, in contrast, seem to chime more with Broszat's method of 'historicization'.

'INTENTIONALISM' AND 'FUNCTIONALISM'*

There is yet another area of controversy that has pitted those who concentrate upon the horrific features of Nazi ideology against those who appeal to general propositions about human behaviour. This debate, which reached its height during the 1980s but still influences much thought about the origins of the Holocaust, concerns the interpretation of the actions that the Nazi regime took towards Jews between the time it came to power in 1933 and the actual beginning of systematic mass murder of Jews in 1941, as well as of the circumstances in which the decision actually to begin mass killing was taken. Some historians have maintained that, even before taking control of Germany, Hitler, following his world-view to its logical consequence and with malice aforethought, had formulated a coherent plan of action intended from the start to bring about the death of each and every Jew within the Third Reich's reach [77; 88; 116]. According to this approach, often labelled 'intentionalist', the succession of anti-Jewish measures undertaken by the Nazi regime in 1933–41 was carefully calculated in advance to facilitate the ultimate goal of total murder. Hitler himself is supposed to have laid out a clear path that would lead Europe's Jews inexorably from social marginalization, political disenfranchisement, and economic ruin to death, while the officials and soldiers of the Third Reich, totally subservient to their sole leader and thoroughly imbued with his fiendish vision, executed that plan flawlessly at every stage.

In contrast, other historians, often called 'functionalists', have contended that when the Nazi regime came to power none of the Third Reich leaders had any clear idea how they were going to act towards the Jews [148; 171]. In their opinion, the idea of systematic mass murder evolved only gradually, a result of the failure of Nazi leaders to find a less brutal way to control the threat to humanity they believed the Jews posed. Often they have presented mass killing as the product of a process of 'cumulative radicalization', born of individual initiatives by Nazi party, government, and military officials undertaken in an administrative climate in which Hitler himself provided little concrete direction [148]. According to this view, Hitler's role in the formulation of the Third Reich's Jewish policies was confined to setting broad guidelines: Reich officials knew that their leader wanted the danger allegedly represented by Jews to be controlled, but they were never told explicitly how they ought to accomplish that goal. As a result, various agencies of the regime experimented with several different anti-Jewish strategies, not always consistent with one another, before the idea of mass killing surfaced. This situation created, in the words of one historian, not a straight path but a 'twisted road to Auschwitz' [171].

Although it was first advanced well before Broszat's plea for historicization, the functionalist argument (of which Broszat was a leading exponent) clearly accords with his call. As Léon Poliakov, a functionalist precursor, wrote, 'to say that the Nazis arrived at genocide as it were in spite of themselves ... reminds us that the Nazis, however criminal they may have been, were only men' [161 *p. 3*]. Some intentionalist historians have perceived in this approach a tendency to trivialize the radical evil in Hitler's exclusion of Jews from the ranks of humanity, claiming that it reduces the murder of millions to the almost accidental outcome of mundane bureaucratic processes. Functionalists have hotly disputed this reading of their position.

Ultimately, though, no matter what the moral implications of each stance, the test of their relative merits must be in the historical record. Is there any documentary trace of a Nazi master-plan for mass murder? Or is there any concrete evidence that the idea was first generated from somewhere within the Nazi administration and not with Hitler?

THE STATE OF DOCUMENTATION

The only formal public statement by the Nazi party of its intentions regarding Jews was contained in the party programme, co-authored by Hitler and adopted in February 1920. That programme, which was reissued unchanged in 1933, called for legislation that would revoke the German citizenship of all Jews; prevent them from voting or holding public office; expel them from Germany if full employment could not be achieved for members of the German race; bar the immigration of Jews from other countries and expel Jewish (and other) immigrants who had entered Germany after August 1914; and prohibit Jews from publishing, investing in, or editing German-language newspapers. It also pledged in general terms that the party would 'fight against the Jewish-materialistic spirit' and declared that 'persons committing base crimes against the People, usurers, profiteers, etc., are to be punished by death without regard to religion or race' [2 *pp. 15–18*].

In light of subsequent events, it is tempting to read into these latter statements a hint of an early design to kill all Jews: usury and profiteering were precisely the sort of 'base crimes' that, according to Hitler, Jewish 'parasites' were racially compelled to perpetrate. Some scholars who incline to this reading have pointed to remarks that Hitler made privately even before writing *Mein Kampf* that seem to have hinted at or spoken explicitly of mass killing. On 16 September 1919 Hitler wrote in a letter that the 'ultimate goal' of state Jewish policy must be not merely 'the elimination of the prerogatives of the Jew which he alone possesses in contradistinction to all other aliens living among us' but 'the elimination of the Jews altogether' [116 *p. 48*]. And in 1922 he reportedly told a journalist that 'once I really am in power, my first and foremost task will be the annihilation of the Jews'; he promised to 'have gallows built in rows' upon which 'the Jews will be hanged indiscriminately ... until all Germany has been cleansed of Jews' [88 *p. 17*].

On the other hand, a leading functionalist historian has wondered whether it is 'not possible that hindsight allows us to see [in such statements] a clarity and a design where they did not exist' [170 *p. 56*]. Did 'elimination of the Jews' (*Entfernung* in German, which could also be translated 'removal' or 'sending away') necessarily imply killing in 1919, or could it have meant expulsion? Indeed, the party platform spoke explicitly of this measure, which, if implemented successfully, would have obviated the need for gallows. Perhaps the 1922 comment about indiscriminate hanging was only hyperbole? After all, in 1935, with the Nazis firmly in power, Hitler told party leaders that he sought merely the enactment of legislation that would ensure 'a tolerable relationship with the Jews living in Germany' and would afford Jews 'opportunities to live their own national life in all areas' [2 *p. 82*]. Was Hitler being disingenuous in one or the other instance? Perhaps his thinking fluctuated over the years. Without appealing anachronistically to the period after 1941, it is difficult to know what any of these statements really meant when they were made or how seriously they were taken.

Besides the 1920 party programme and Hitler's scattered and perhaps inconsistent statements about practical measures that would eliminate the Jewish danger as he perceived it, a number of Nazi officials devised their own plans for dealing with the Jews. One was put forward in April 1933 by a 'working group' of eight administrators and advisers, chaired by jurist Rudolf Becker and including the head of the Prussian Gestapo, Rudolf Diels. This proposal called for the compulsory enrolment of all German Jews in an Association of Jews in Germany, to be governed by a Jewish Council (*Judenrat**) and supervised by a state-appointed 'people's guardian' (*Volkswart*), whose job was both 'to protect the German people from the danger posed by Jewry' and 'to protect the Jews and secure their rights'. In discharging the former function the *Volkswart* was 'empowered to take any measures that seem necessary for the protection of German citizens against Jewish abuse of laws and economic power'. Jews were to be excluded from the military and civil service; denied the vote; restricted in access to the free professions; and forbidden from serving as directors of large banks, public utilities, or cultural institutions, as editors of German periodicals, or as schoolteachers. Marriages and extramarital sexual relations between Jews and non-Jews were to be banned. Jews who had become naturalized in Germany after August 1914 were to lose their citizenship and be expelled from the country, as were all foreign Jews. All German Jews were to be 'officially obliged to add the letter J to their surnames' [1 *pp. 45, 47, 53*]. This plan, then, looked to legislation to isolate Jews from Germany society without necessarily doing them physical harm.

Another statement of policy was prepared in January 1939 by the German foreign ministry. This document declared that 'the ultimate aim of Germany's Jewish policy is the emigration of all Jews living in German territory'. According to the statement, emigration was to be induced through the forced liquidation of Jewish businesses and expropriation of Jewish property, which would make it impossible for Jews to survive in Germany economically. However, the document noted that 'the Jewish question will not be solved when the last Jew has left German soil'. It anticipated that an influx of Jewish refugees into other lands would 'waken the interest in ... the Jewish danger in many countries', so that 'the Jewish question will develop' into an international political problem'. Eventually, it was hoped, all the nations of the world would allocate a small part of the globe for a 'Jewish reservation'*, where Jews, isolated from the rest of humanity, would no longer threaten 'the national character of the nations' [2 *pp. 127, 129, 131*]. Germany, in other words, would not eliminate the putative Jewish threat to mankind by its own action but would merely spark other governments to move against it.

Yet another indication of the regime's thinking about what to do with Jews was contained in an 'express letter' by Reinhard Heydrich*, chief of the Security Police, issued on 21 September 1939. Written three weeks after the German invasion of Poland that launched the Second World War, this memorandum discussed the disposition of the more than 2 million Polish Jews about to fall under German rule. It outlined three fundamental measures to be taken immediately: concentration of Jews from the countryside into larger cities near rail lines; establishment of a Jewish Council in each community, to be responsible for implementing all future German directives and for conducting a census of all Jews by age, sex, and occupation; and expropriation of Jewish businesses and property to the extent local economic conditions permitted. However, it spoke of these measures merely as means to a 'final aim' (*Endziel*), which would 'require extended periods of time' for completion and was 'to be kept strictly secret' [2 *pp. 173–8*].

Intentionalist historians have interpreted the reference to a secret 'final aim' as proof that 'a master plan for annihilating the Jews had already been conceived, though only the preliminary stages were now to be implemented' [77 *p. 116*]. In their view, it was no coincidence that Heydrich issued his memorandum almost simultaneously with the outbreak of war: Hitler had long intended to kill all Jews, but he needed the chaos of war to camouflage his murderous acts. They argue that Hitler closely associated the war against Poland with the war against the Jews in his own mind: indeed, in a speech to the Reichstag on 30 January 1939 he had warned that 'if the international Jewish financiers in and outside Europe should succeed in plunging the nations ... into a world war, the result will be ... the annihilation of the Jewish race in Europe' [2 *pp. 134–5*]. Functionalist historians, on the other hand, noting that Heydrich's memorandum did not mention killing explicitly, have contended that the 'final aim' referred to the 'Jewish reservation' that the foreign ministry had discussed seven months earlier. They point out that when Heydrich issued his 'express letter', and for over a year thereafter, high officials in both the foreign ministry and Heydrich's own security service were developing two plans to create such a reservation, one in the area around the Polish city of Lublin, the other on the island of Madagascar* [51; 95]. On 25 May 1940 Heydrich's superior, Heinrich Himmler, the person in charge of all security forces throughout the Reich (later to become the chief supervisor of mass killing), wrote that he hoped that 'Jews will be completely extinguished through ... large-scale emigration ... to Africa or some other colony' [2 *p. 198*]. On 3 July 1940 several government departments approved a plan by which Madagascar would be made available 'for the solution of the Jewish question', holding Europe's Jews 'in German hands as a pledge for the future good behaviour of the members of their race in America' [2 *pp. 217–18*]. Hence one historian has concluded that, far from being 'indicative of a mass-murder plan', Heydrich's memorandum actually contained 'a brutal plan ... to facilitate a later massive expulsion' [51 *p. 42*].

Lucy Dawidowicz, an ardent intentionalist, tried to refute the functionalist reading, arguing that 'everything we know of National Socialist ideology precludes our accepting ... a Jewish reservation as the last stage of the Final Solution'. In her view, that ideology required that all Jews be killed; hence 'a reservation could have been conceived of only as a transitional stage' on the road to mass murder [77 *p. 118*]. On the other hand, Yehuda Bauer has suggested that 'although mass murder of the Jews was the logical consequence of Nazi theories ..., that logical conclusion was not drawn until 1941' [51 *p. 45*]. In the end, though, neither position can be proved conclusively by reference to the documentary record. To date no document has been found that refers explicitly to a mass murder plan in a way that leaves no room for conflicting interpretations. For this reason, it is also impossible to determine with certainty when mass murder became the regime's preferred course of action towards Jews or where within the regime the initiative for mass murder originated.

A STEP-BY-STEP PROCESS?

Because of the lack of unambiguous documentation, much of the intentionalist–functionalist debate has focused upon whether a preconceived murder plan can be inferred from the specific actions the German regime took towards Jews before the actual onset of mass killing in June 1941.

The idea that those actions constituted a step-by-step 'destruction process' was first advanced by Raul Hilberg in 1961. Hilberg identified four sequential stages in this process: definition, expropriation, concentration, and annihilation, each implemented by professional bureaucrats doing a job assigned by their superiors.

Definition of Jews, according to Hilberg, began in April 1933. On 7 April the Reich enacted a Law for the Restoration of the Professional Civil Service*, which provided that 'civil servants who are not of Aryan descent are to be retired' [2 *p. 40*]. Four days later, an amendment to the law declared that 'a person is to be considered non-Aryan if he is descended from non-Aryan, and especially from Jewish parents or grandparents. It is sufficient if one parent or grandparent is non-Aryan. This is to be assumed ... where one parent or grandparent was of the Jewish religion' [2 *p. 41*]. The definition was refined following the September 1935 enactment of the Law on Reich Citizenship and the Law for the Protection of German Blood and Honour – the so-called Nuremberg Laws [2 *pp. 77–9*]. According to the First Regulation to the Reich Citizenship Law, proclaimed on 14 November 1935, 'a Jew is a person descended from at least three grandparents who are full Jews by race' [2 *p. 80*]. The regulation also provided that persons descended from only two Jewish grandparents would be considered Jews if they were members of a Jewish religious community, married to a Jew, or born of one Jewish parent after the Nuremberg Laws had been promulgated. Persons with one or two Jewish grandparents who did not meet any of these conditions eventually became known as *Mischlinge** (people of mixed blood); although technically non-Aryans and subject to some legal discrimination, they were not placed under the sentence of death that eventually befell Jews.

Expropriation involved measures that stripped Jews of their livelihoods, property, and financial reserves. This process began in 1933, with the civil service law and the dismissal of many Jews from positions in German academic and cultural institutions. It continued sporadically through 1937, as many Jewish business owners were pressured (often under threat of physical force) to sell their enterprises to non-Jews at a fraction of their value. In 1938 concrete steps were taken towards full-scale removal of Jews from the German economy. On 26 April 1938 all German Jews were compelled to register their assets. Jewish doctors were forbidden to treat non-Jewish patients on 25 July; Jewish lawyers were disbarred on 27 September. On 12 November all Jewish retail businesses were ordered liquidated; proprietors were forced to sell their stock to government-approved buyers at fixed prices. Finally, a law of 3 December empowered the government to appoint trustees for Jewish-owned industrial enterprises, whose function was to dissolve Jewish establishments or transfer them to non-Jewish hands. Jews' remaining savings were placed in blocked accounts from which they could draw only a fixed subsistence allowance [44].

Concentration meant, in the first instance, visibly separating Jews from non-Jews. Separation measures commenced with the 1935 Law for the Protection of German Blood and Honour (the second Nuremberg Law), which forbade marriage or extramarital sexual relations between Jews and non-Jews. As with expropriation, however, the process began in earnest only in 1938. Beginning in July, Jews' identity papers and passports were marked with a special sign. On 17 August an ordinance required all Jews without identifiably Jewish first names to add a middle name of Israel or Sara. In November new laws barred Jews from receiving medical treatment except in Jewish hospitals and expelled Jewish children from state schools. The following month housing restrictions were imposed, with Jews permitted to live only in specially designated apartment buildings.

Concentration took on an additional meaning in Poland following Germany's conquest of that country in September 1939. On 23

November 1939 the German Governor General of occupied Poland, Hans Frank, ordered 'all Jews ... to wear on the right sleeve ... a white band ... with the Star of David on it' [2 p. *178*]. Moreover, the Heydrich memorandum of 21 September 1939 called for 'Jewish communities of less than 500 persons ... to be dissolved and transferred' to 'cities located on railroad lines'. It also suggested that 'the concentration of the Jews in the cities will probably call for regulations ... which will forbid their entry into certain quarters' and require them 'not [to] leave the ghetto' [2 *pp. 174–5*]. Indeed, between October 1939 and April 1941 special closed areas, called 'ghettos' or 'Jewish residential quarters', were established in most occupied Polish cities and towns. Most ghettos were surrounded by high walls and gates that could not be crossed without special permission; they both constrained Jews' physical ability to manoeuvre and isolated them from the surrounding Polish population.

It seems logical to assume that each of the first three steps in Hilberg's 'destruction process' brought the final step of annihilation closer. But the ability to discern a step-by-step destruction process in hindsight has not resolved the intentionalist–functionalist debate. For one thing, definition, expropriation, and concentration do not represent everything done to Jews under Nazi rule. From the time the Nazis came to power Jews were subjected to periodic street violence and terror. Newspapers constantly published vituperative articles about Jews. Schoolchildren were taught that Jews were a danger to humanity. Pickets regularly stood outside Jewish shops, warning customers not to buy from Jews. On 1 April 1933 the regime proclaimed a nationwide boycott of Jewish businesses. On 9 June 1938 German authorities ordered the main synagogue in Munich destroyed; the Nuremberg synagogue was demolished on 10 August. On 9–10 November 1938, the so-called 'night of the broken glass' (Kristallnacht), Nazi party leaders instigated riots throughout Germany, in which 1,400 synagogues and 7,500 Jewish-owned shops were attacked and looted and 91 Jews killed.

Intentionalist and functionalist historians differ over how to interpret these brutal Nazi anti-Jewish actions (which Hilberg excluded from his destruction process on the grounds that they did not materially advance eventual mass killing), just as they differ over how to interpret measures aimed at definition, expropriation, and concentration. Intentionalist historians tend to view brutality, boycott, legislation, and ghettoization all as parts of a single campaign, orchestrated by Hitler, 'to turn the Jews into "socially dead" beings' before murdering them [100 p. *135*]. Functionalists, in contrast, often argue that the wide variety of anti-Jewish actions demonstrates that Jewish policy was controlled by no single clear authoritative vision, of Hitler or of anyone else: 'the gruesome efficiency of the ... death camps came only after the voices of numerous contestants for control over Jewish policy had been silenced' [171 *p. 260*]. For them, the idea of a step-by-step destruction process represents a scholar's retrospective imposition of order upon a situation that contemporaries experienced as chaotic.

Moreover, as Hilberg himself recognized, the steps of definition, expropriation, and concentration could have served the goal of expulsion just as easily as they eventually served the goal of murder. Thus he did not infer a prior murder plan from his analysis. The decision to begin systematic mass killing of Jews, he suggested, was not taken until the destruction process had already reached an advanced stage; until that time the German government retained a number of possible options for dealing with the ostensible Jewish threat.

JEWISH POLICY AND GLOBAL STRATEGY

One way to resolve these conflicting interpretations is to recall the difference between aspirations and policy. It may be that even before coming to power Hitler believed that the only effective way to remove the threat to humanity that Jews represented in his world-view was to kill them all, and he may have aspired to this long-range goal. But even so, he may not have had any clear idea about when or how the goal could be achieved. It is also possible that not many others shared the goal initially and that Hitler was not able to impose it unilaterally on the Nazi regime. Perhaps at first he regarded his aspiration as utopian and thus not worth formulating as an immediate policy aim.

One reason that Hitler might have thought this way is that in 1933 less than 4 per cent of the world's Jews and less than 8 per cent of the Jews of Europe were under Nazi control. The 2.3 million Jews in Austria, the Czech lands, and western Poland came under German occupation only in 1938–39; 300,000 in occupied France, the Benelux countries, and Norway in 1940; and 4.4 million in eastern Poland, the Soviet Union, the Baltic states, Serbia, and Greece in 1941. Another 1.8 million Jews lived in countries that became allied with Nazi Germany between 1939 and 1941: Slovakia, Vichy France, Italy, Romania, Hungary, Bulgaria, and Croatia. In other words, even had he so wished, Hitler had no chance to eliminate the Jewish threat even in Europe (let alone throughout the world) until 1941. Until then, Nazi Jewish policy could pursue more limited, palliative objectives, like eliminating contact between Jews and Germans, plundering Jewish assets, or providing psychological release for fanatical Jew-haters, while keeping open the option of total murder for a time when Germany controlled many more Jews.

At first glance, the policy of emigration enunciated in the January 1939 foreign ministry memorandum appears to contradict this reasoning, because it implied removing Jews from Germany's control. Indeed, pushing Jews out – now more and more by force – was the policy Germany most actively pursued following the March 1938 annexation of Austria [183]. On 26 August 1938 Reich authorities established a Central Office for Jewish Emigration* in Vienna, whose purpose was to streamline procedures for obtaining passports and visas. A similar office was opened in Prague after Germany overran Czechoslovakia in March 1939 and in other Reich cities thereafter. Simultaneously the Jews of those countries were subjected to ongoing violence and terror to frighten them into leaving; some Jews were even threatened with imprisonment if they did not emigrate. As a result, some 290,000 Jews left Reich-controlled territories in 1938–39, in addition to the 129,000 who had left in 1933–37. If Hitler intended ultimately to kill these Jews, why did he let them go?

One answer, suggested by Eberhard Jäckel, is that there was a basic contradiction in Hitler's thinking: 'as a German he wanted the elimination of the German Jews before all others', even as in the long term he wished to 'do ... humanity a service by exterminating' all Jews everywhere [115 *p. 48*]. Another possibility may lie in Hitler's foreign policy, whose key aim was to conquer the Soviet Union, thereby enlarging Germany's 'living space' and eliminating the spectre of Bolshevism. Achieving that aim required Germany to build up its economic and military power and to expand its territorial base eastward. The economic-military build-up began in earnest with the launching of the Four-Year Plan in 1936; territorial expansion began with the Austrian annexation in 1938. However, both actions involved violations of the Versailles Treaty that Germany had signed after the First World War. Germany thus needed to take care lest Britain or France, the other major parties to the treaty, intervene militarily to punish its infractions and nip its global strategy in the bud. Keeping the western powers at bay while Germany became the dominant force in continental Europe was a serious challenge for German politicians, and they employed many sophisticated devices to meet it [113].

One way of discouraging western military intervention against Germany was to portray intervention as serving nefarious Jewish interests. Indeed, from 1933 the Nazi regime strove to isolate Jews in world public opinion, depicting 'international financial Jewry' as determined to plunge Britain and France into war against a Germany that had no aggressive intentions towards them. The emigration policy might well have been part of this strategy. As the January 1939 foreign ministry memorandum indicated, 'the greater the burden [the Jewish immigrant] constitutes for the country [of immigration] ..., the stronger the reaction ... and the more desirable the effect in support of German propaganda' [2 *p. 131*]. By arousing fear in western countries of a massive influx of penniless Jewish refugees, Germany may have hoped to induce western governments to turn away Jews from their domains. German propagandists could then warn the public in those countries against going to war in the interests of people whom they themselves did not want as neighbours. Hitler himself spoke in this fashion in his Reichstag speech of 30 January 1939: 'The nations are no longer willing to die on the battlefield so that this unstable international race may profiteer from a war' [2 *p. 135*]. And if some German Jews should manage through emigration to escape the Nazis' reach, the boon to Germany's global strategy that the emigration policy stood to yield by cultivating western public reluctance to stop German rearmament and eastward expansion may have more than compensated for this loss.

This analysis, which permits the notion of Hitler's constant intention to kill Jews *en masse* to be reconciled with the picture of the 'twisted road', is hypothetical; no documents uncovered to date can prove or disprove its validity. As a result, the intentionalist–functionalist controversy is not likely ever to be conclusively resolved. Nonetheless, it has become increasingly clear that without Hitler's insistence that a way be found to eliminate what his world-view taught him was the mortal danger Jews posed to humanity, the destruction process that can be identified in hindsight would never have been set in motion. Whether Hitler or other elements of the Nazi regime first set it in motion and propelled it along its course, whether the end of that course was always clear to those who maintained it, whether it was the product of evil design or of the normal workings of a bureaucracy – these are problems of interpretation about which scholars will continue to disagree.

5   RESPONDING TO PERSECUTION

If historians have found it difficult to ascertain precisely how the Nazi regime planned to deal with the Jews within its reach at any given moment between 1933 and 1941, how much more challenging must it have been for contemporaries to do so. Hindsight easily creates the impression that the encounter between the Third Reich and the Jews had to unfold as it ultimately did, prompting the question of why observers did not see the handwriting on the wall until it was too late. For two decades and more following the Holocaust such hindsight informed much of the writing on responses to Nazi rule. The Jews of Germany in particular were often chided for their alleged 'psychological predisposition against contemplating any alternative to the favourable and seemingly promising situation' they enjoyed on the eve of the Nazi era [149 *p. 8*]. Also, the actions of bystanders to the encounter between the Third Reich and the Jews in the 1930s have been interpreted in light of the systematic mass killing that characterized that encounter only after 1941. More recently, though, many historians have rejected this approach, noting that it assumes that there was always a clear message on the wall to be read, that the message always spelled death, and that any alert and reasonably intelligent observer should have been able to read it at any time. In the event, the first two assumptions have already been shown to be questionable. The third is no less problematic.

PERCEIVING THE THREAT

Even if the intentionalist position is correct and a master-plan for systematic killing of all Jews within the Third Reich's reach had been set in motion from the time the Nazis acceded to power, the existence of such a plan was never made public. Thus all those not privy to the regime's internal, behind-the-scenes discussions of Jewish matters could only try to infer its long-range intentions indirectly, from what they were able to observe of its actual behaviour towards Jews. And what was observable – especially before the pace of expropriation and concentration measures and of government-sponsored violence surged in 1938 – was subject to many possible interpretations.

To be sure, the economic and social conditions of day-to-day life for German Jewry deteriorated steadily from 1933 on. Mounting unemployment resulting from job dismissals and expropriation measures brought widespread poverty. By 1936 over 20 per cent of German Jews were dependent on welfare; another 20–25 per cent lived on savings; while only 10–15 per cent were estimated able to earn a comfortable living [44]. Out of 1,600 Jewish communities in Germany in 1933, 200 had dissolved by 1937, and another 600 were able to remain solvent only with outside assistance. Landlords increasingly refused to rent to Jews, storekeepers to sell them food and clothing. Many Jews' relations with non-Jewish friends became increasingly strained, and Jewish schoolchildren, though permitted to attend German state schools, were subjected to constant harassment by teachers and fellow students [117].

But there were also mitigating facts to be observed. True, for several months following Hitler's appointment as German Chancellor on 30 January 1933, units of Nazi storm troopers (SA) perpetrated numerous acts of violence against Jews; but state authorities often suppressed these actions, fearing the general threat to public order they posed, and violence subsided between 1934 and 1938 [171]. Concentration camps* had been built beginning in 1933, but until 1938 they were used mainly against political dissidents; communists, in particular, seemed to bear the brunt of the regime's most brutal repressive measures, not Jews. Jews had been excluded from the German army in early 1934, but as late as August 1935 Jewish veterans were receiving decorations for past service. Jewish newspapers continued to be sold in public and even to challenge the regime until October 1935. In 1936 the government promised unrestricted freedom to Jewish artists as long as they confined themselves to 'Jewish' themes. Random kindnesses and quiet expressions of sympathy for Jews by Germans were not uncommon. As late as 1939 Jews were sometimes able to find redress for their grievances against non-Jews in German courts. Many Germans, including Nazi party members, continued to do business with Jews well into the 1930s, ignoring widespread admonitions against such behaviour; some top Nazi officials were even patronizing Jewish-owned hotels until 1938. In the same year, five Jews were still directors of at least one major German bank [92; 117]. And for a number of Jews who owned large businesses and factories, the general upswing in the German economy during the mid-1930s actually proved a financial boon [176].

Moreover, the first years of Nazi rule were experienced differently by different Jews, depending upon their age, sex, class, occupation, place of residence, and political affiliation. Small-town Jews often became victims of economic pressure, social ostracism, and violence earlier and more consistently than city dwellers. Wealthier Jews often had the means to circumvent restrictions or to compensate for them in ways unavailable to their less well-to-do co-religionists. Women tended to suffer less abuse by state officials than men, but they were often more exposed to hostile interactions with non-Jews in the private sphere. Jews active in left-wing political movements confronted the most brutal aspects of the regime from the outset, whereas others could at first feel themselves relatively safe from arbitrary search and arrest [117].

What could be deduced from such conflicting and confusing signals about German long-range plans? Understandably, Jewish assessments were mixed. Most agreed that the situation represented an 'end of emancipation', in which Jews would no longer be regarded as equal citizens of Germany or as rightful members of German society. But where some perceived rightlessness from the start as a prelude to what Jewish banker Georg Solmssen called 'the economic and moral annihilation of all members, without any distinctions, of the Jewish race living in Germany' [92 *p. 35*], many more took comfort in the thought that 'Jewry has long undergone a process ... of constant fluctuation between the poles of emancipation and ghettoization' [17 *p. 174*], suggesting that Jewish rights and status would eventually be restored. As the popular German Jewish novelist Lion Feuchtwanger wrote after the promulgation of the Nuremberg Laws, '[T]hrough the ... study of history I have reached the ... conviction that ... we cannot consider an eruption of madness such as the one in Germany as something that can last more than a generation' [92 *p. 174*]. In the early years of Nazi rule some thought they saw signs that the regime was on the verge of collapse, and with it all official discrimination and persecution. Others interpreted Hitler's 1935 statement that he sought 'opportunities [for Jews] to live their own national life in all areas' as indicating that the regime sought merely to regulate Jews as a minority while allowing them broad internal autonomy, according to the model that had prevailed in medieval Europe [*Doc. 5*].

In the end, German Jews could never be completely sure of the government's intentions. In November 1933 the Organization of Independent Orthodox Communities sent a memorandum to Hitler asking him to 'tell us the truth openly' about what lay in store. On the one hand, the memorandum explained, 'the position of German Jewry must be perceived as altogether desperate ..., and ... the German National Government might all too easily be suspected of aiming deliberately at [its] destruction'. On the other hand, it declared, 'Orthodox Jewry is unwilling to abandon the conviction that it is not the aim of the German Government to destroy the German Jews'. Thus, it stated, 'if we should be mistaken, if you ... have indeed set [yourself] the ultimate aim of the elimination of German Jewry ..., then we do not wish to cling to illusions any longer and would prefer to know the bitter truth' [2 *p. 61*]. Hitler offered no response; the uncertainty remained.

Some outside observers, like the American radio correspondent William L. Shirer, thought German Jews 'unduly optimistic' [28 *p. 31*]. But even the most pessimistic commentators, Jewish and non-Jewish alike, foresaw no more than economic ruin and spiritual breakdown, which might eventually force Jews out of Germany altogether. This is what phrases like 'destruction', 'elimination', and 'annihilation' meant to virtually everyone at the time, not systematic mass killing. A careful reading of *Mein Kampf* might, perhaps, have led to a more radical prognosis; but, as historian Jacob Katz observed, 'an essential difference exists between announcing an intention and resolving to act upon it. Nobody, including Hitler himself, could know whether he would ever have the opportunity to carry out his intentions and how far he would go [if he did]' [119 *p. 43*].

TO LEAVE OR NOT TO LEAVE?

However varied their perceptions of the threat facing them, virtually all German Jews acknowledged that life under the Nazi regime would be hard. In theory it was possible to avoid hardship altogether through emigration. Indeed, many German Jews left: 37,000 in 1933, 23,000 in 1934, 21,000 in 1935, 25,000 in 1936, and 23,000 in 1937. But these represented only about one-quarter of the 525,000 Jews living in Germany in 1933. It was only after the German government placed emigration at the centre of its Jewish policy following the annexation of Austria in 1938 and stepped up economic and physical pressure accordingly that a majority of German Jews sought to flee the country [177]. Thus it is often asked why more did not seek to leave sooner.

The answer is that emigration had serious costs. Some were literal: a steep 'flight tax' was imposed on the property of those who sought to leave, and the transfer of assets abroad was severely restricted.

Others were less tangible. Emigration meant the pain of leaving behind family, friends, and a familiar environment to which most German Jews felt a deep attachment. It also meant economic insecurity. Migrants often arrived at their destinations without means of support or skills that could be transferred easily to their new environment, and with much of the world still suffering from the economic depression of the 1930s, employment opportunities were scarce. Migrants unable to work in their professions or to support themselves at all lost social status as well, and their sense of personal identity was often shaken. Such difficulties led some 10,000 Jews who had fled Germany in the first months after the Nazis took power to return by early 1935; only a government threat to incarcerate returnees in concentration camps put an end to this reverse migration.

Whether these costs were worth bearing depended both upon how severely individual Jews were likely to feel them and upon how they assessed the severity of the Nazi threat. Research by historian Marion Kaplan suggests that women, whose status was less defined by their jobs than men's and who viewed the situation more from the perspective of everyday life than from that of high politics, tended more towards pessimism than men and were more willing to uproot themselves [117] [*Doc. 6*]. But with the increasing tempo of expropriation, concentration, and terror during 1938, and especially after the Kristallnacht riots in November, differences in perception narrowed, and the desire to emigrate became virtually universal. Some 40,000 German Jews fled the country in 1938, 78,000 in 1939; thousands more wished to leave but found they had no means to do so or no place to go. Migration and natural decrease lowered Germany's Jewish population to under 200,000 by the outbreak of war; those who remained were disproportionately elderly or ill.

COMMUNAL LEADERSHIP: COPING AND RESISTING

Because emigration was not immediate and total, German Jews, even those who remained under Nazi rule only a short time before fleeing, needed help coping with their situation. The burden of helping fell largely upon German Jewish welfare organizations. In April 1933 a coalition of Jewish groups created a countrywide Central Committee for Aid and Reconstruction. This Committee tried to find jobs for Jews who had lost them and offered interest-free loans to help shopkeepers remain afloat. In October 1935 a Jewish Winter Aid campaign provided food, clothing, and shelter for almost 85,000 Jews – 20 per cent of German Jewry at the time [127; 130]. A Jewish Cultural

Association, founded in 1933, offered employment to many Jewish artists and intellectuals who had been dismissed from their positions soon following the Nazi take-over. One Jewish scholar and communal leader summarized the spirit that underlay these activities: 'They can condemn us to hunger, but they cannot condemn us to starvation' [92 *p. 62*].

Additionally, a central Jewish political representation, the Reichsvertretung*, formed in September 1933, sought to provide Jews with a unified voice in the public arena. Besides supervising welfare work, this body interceded with state authorities on behalf of individual Jews and lobbied for the most lenient application possible of anti-Jewish laws. It vigorously protested defamatory statements made in the press and by public officials, hoping to defend 'the honour of the Jewish name' [2 *p. 59*]. And, as the situation for Jewish children in state schools became untenable, the Reichsvertretung organized Jewish schools. By 1937, some 24,000 elementary and secondary school pupils, representing 61 per cent of the Jewish school-age population, attended 160 Reichsvertretung educational institutions [75].

Historians are divided over how effectively the Reichsvertretung provided leadership to German Jews. Some have suggested that its perception of the Nazi threat was as flawed as that of most German Jews and less accurate than that of many; had it been otherwise, the organization would have actively encouraged immediate mass emigration instead of concentrating upon palliative measures [139; 156]. Others contend that the Reichsvertretung understood by 1935 that any tolerable existence for Jews under Nazi rule was impossible and accepted 'the necessity for emigration on a large scale' [130 *p. 146*]. In the event, the Reichsvertretung actively assisted many Jews who wished to leave Germany in paying the flight tax, and it conducted training courses to help would-be emigrants learn the skills they would need for successful relocation; but it never recommended formally that German Jews should leave *en masse*. This does not mean that its prognosis was more optimistic than the observable facts warranted. German Jewish leaders faced a conundrum over emigration. They were troubled not only by the regime's anti-Jewish actions but by its constant branding of Jews as enemies of Germany. For German Jews who had worked assiduously during the previous century to eliminate the cultural barriers that had set them apart from the surrounding society and had cultivated a strong sense of themselves as Germans, this was an especially painful – sometimes even a psychologically unbearable – charge [*Doc. 7*]. In this context, active official Jewish encouragement of mass emigration could have been understood as confirming the regime's position that Jews had no place in Germany's future. In other words, emigration *en masse* was easily interpreted as abandoning the battle for Jewish rights. Joining that battle, in contrast, could be taken as the path of heroic resistance; it meant trying defiantly to thwart what even the most pessimistic contemporary observers saw as the Nazis' ultimate aim – the banishment of Jews from German life. Hence the Central Committee for Aid and Reconstruction publicly proclaimed that 'there is no honour in leaving Germany in order to live untroubled on your income abroad, free of the fate of your brothers', urging German Jews to 'do your duty here' [2 *pp. 49–50*].

Frequently the public proclamations of German Jewish leaders also stressed the necessity to show pride in Jewishness. Following the anti-Jewish boycott of 1 April 1933, in which Jewish-owned shops were marked with a yellow Star of David, a leading Jewish newspaper urged Jews to remember that this symbol had once adorned the shield of King David and thus to turn the derogatory sign into 'a badge of honour' [2 *p. 46*]. In order to foster such pride, the Reichsvertretung encouraged Jewish adults to learn more about their heritage. Under its auspices the philosopher Martin Buber opened a Central Office for Jewish Adult Education, whose purpose was to 'groom a community that will stand firm, that will prevail, that will guard the spark' of Jewish culture [6 *p. 161*]. These efforts appear to have found considerable response among German Jews, who felt that since they had been 'singled out for persecution ... solely because they were Jews, it was necessary that their Judaism be invested with powerful meaning and sufficient inspirational power to enable them to endure the burden of hate and hardship' [140 *p. 105; Doc. 8*].

Yet sponsoring such 'spiritual resistance' did not necessarily work against emigration, as some have charged [41]. On the contrary, the widespread 'return to Judaism' among German Jews led in many cases to increasing identification with Zionism and interest in the possibility of resettlement in Palestine. Indeed, almost 30 per cent of the Jews who left Germany in 1933–35 went to that country, many as a result of new-found Jewish ethnic consciousness and nationalist convictions. Membership in Zionist organizations also increased exponentially during those years [134].

ZIONISM, GERMAN JEWRY, AND WORLD JEWRY

Although before 1933 Zionism had attracted only a small minority of German Jews, and most German Jewish leaders had regarded its nationalist message as inimical to the idea of emancipation, after the Nazi rise to power Zionists became part of the Reichsvertretung, and even Germany's largest Jewish organization, which had long insisted that Jews constituted a religious group only, acknowledged that 'Palestine holds a special place among the countries of immigration' and that 'Palestine is an essential factor in [Jewry's] survival' [6 *p. 167*]. This development was eventually to offset much of the reluctance of non-Zionist Jewish leaders to encourage Jews to leave.

Zionists, both in and out of Germany, were among the first to call upon German Jewry to make emigration (to Palestine) a communal priority. Chaim Arlosoroff*, head of the Political Department of the Jewish Agency for Palestine*, who visited Germany in April 1933, argued that although Palestine might not provide the sole solution to German Jewry's predicament, it had the advantage of permanence. Arlosoroff also suggested that Zionists might actually be able to reach an agreement with the Nazi regime that would allow Jews emigrating to Palestine to take a significant portion of their assets with them; he proposed that departing Jews be allowed to use the value of the assets they left behind to purchase German-made goods exported to the Middle East. Such an agreement, he thought, could help resettle large numbers of German Jews within three or four years [*Doc. 9*].

There were several bases for this optimism. First, many Zionists thought that their movement and the Nazis shared a common interest in seeing Jews leave Germany. Second, they understood that the German economy, hard-hit by the depression of the early 1930s, was in dire straits; indeed, the German government needed desperately to develop export markets for German industries, in order to build foreign currency reserves and provide jobs for millions of unemployed Germans. Finally, they knew that, unlike much of the world, the economy of Jewish Palestine was booming and that there was significant demand there for heavy machinery, which could be obtained from manufacturers in several countries, not only Germany. They believed, therefore, that they possessed both ideological and economic leverage that they, alone among Jewish leaders, could exercise to Jewish advantage [54; 154].

As it happened, individual Zionists from Germany and Palestine had been speaking informally with certain German officials along these lines even before Arlosoroff had broached his idea publicly. Negotiations were institutionalized in May 1933, and on 17 August a formal agreement was actually concluded between the German Zionist Federation and the German Ministry of Economic Affairs. Known (even in German) by the Hebrew name Haavara* (transfer), the arrangement permitted prospective emigrants to invest in a new export company, which would buy German merchandise and market it in the Middle East. Payments for merchandise sold would be sent to a special account in a Palestine bank. When emigrants who had invested in the export company reached Palestine, they could redeem their shares at the bank and receive cash out of the special account. The agreement was actually implemented, too: by 1939, 50,000 German Jews had transfered £8 million to Palestine [134; 154].

Haavara was widely supported by German Jews, Zionist and non-Zionist alike. In 1937 the Reichsvertretung even reached agreement with the government to make similar arrangements for Jews departing for other countries [54; 177]. But many Jews outside Germany, Zionists and non-Zionists, opposed it. In March 1933, before the negotiations that led to Haavara had begun, Jews in several countries had adopted a radically different response to the threat of Nazi persecution of their German co-religionists: they had organized a boycott of German products, hoping to thwart Nazi efforts to solve Germany's economic problems and thereby encourage internal German opposition to the Nazi regime. Nazi officials feared that such a boycott could do Germany real economic harm, and they resolved to fight it: on 25 March 1933, Interior Minister Hermann Goering ordered German Jewish leaders to tell their counterparts in Britain and the United States that continuation of the boycott or other anti-Nazi agitation would be met with reprisals against German Jews. In fact, the German anti-Jewish boycott of 1 April 1933 was represented as retaliation for the Jewish anti-German boycott abroad. German Jewish leaders delivered the message, urging that the boycott cease. Nevertheless, over the next several months the boycott movement gained strength among world Jewry [103; 144; 182].

Haavara, which favoured negotiation over confrontation, clearly represented the antithesis of the boycott strategy and threatened to defeat it. As a result, it was attacked vigorously by many non-German Jews. It was also opposed on moral grounds: by promoting German exports, the agreement helped strengthen a regime that was persecuting Jews [191]. This controversy has continued in retrospect, with historians and others hotly debating whether Haavara undermined a real chance to nip the Nazi threat in the bud. Careful statistical analysis of both the boycott and Haavara suggest, however, that neither had more than a minuscule effect on the German economy [45; 54]. German officials may have feared the boycott at first, but it appears that they supported Haavara less because of its economic potential and more because it represented a way to rid Germany of many Jews. At least some agencies of the Nazi regime appear to have pursued this goal even in 1933, as long as it could be accomplished without disrupting the economy. Measures such as the 'flight tax' and restrictions on the removal of property were supposed to prevent disruption, but they also discouraged Jews from emigrating. Haavara thus removed both a source of discouragement for Jews and one of economic loss for Germany.

EXTERNAL OBSTACLES TO EMIGRATION

As time progressed, however, it became clear that there were other obstacles to emigration that neither Nazis nor Jews could eliminate. These were hurdles imposed by countries receiving German Jewish refugees.

By the early 1930s, virtually all countries possessed legal and administrative means of restricting immigration, and with much of the world suffering economic depression, most thought it wise to employ them. True, in a widespread outpouring of sympathy immediately following the Nazi take-over, several European states chose temporarily not to do so, thereby allowing almost 30,000 German Jews to enter their borders in 1933. That sympathy dissipated, however, as it became clear that the Nazi government was likely to last, and by 1935 officials in the most likely receiving countries were actively trying to hold the refugee flow to a minimum. Some governments expressed concern about setting a dangerous precedent: certain eastern European countries were, for their own reasons, pressuring their much greater numbers of Jews to emigrate, and if restrictions were relaxed for German Jews, would not Jews from these other countries also demand similar consideration? [142; 172; 176]

Until 1936 Palestine represented an exception to this thinking. Britain governed Palestine under a League of Nations mandate that required it to promote the development of a Jewish national home by facilitating Jewish immigration. In theory Britain limited the number of immigrants according to the country's 'economic absorptive capacity', but with the Palestinian economy growing, this restriction meant little in practice. For this reason, too, Palestine was an attractive destination, not only for German Jews but for Jews leaving eastern Europe as well. Where in 1932 fewer than 10,000 Jews had migrated to Palestine, the number rose to 30,327 in 1933, 42,359 in 1934, and 61,854 in 1935, with the overall Jewish population of the country increasing 80 per cent in that interval. That growth worried local Arab leaders, who feared that Jews would soon become a majority. In

April 1936 Palestinian Arabs launched a revolt against British rule and Jewish settlement, which eventually tied down two army divisions (40 per cent of Britain's battle-ready forces) in maintaining order. To free those troops for use in potential trouble-spots elsewhere around the globe, Britain tried to assuage Arab grievances; in 1937 it began limiting Jewish immigration to 1,000 per month. As a result only half as many German Jews entered Palestine in 1937–38 as had in 1933–34 [74].

Slowing the flow of refugees to Palestine merely increased demand for admission to other destinations, however – a phenomenon that led Britain, France, the United States, and other potential receiving countries to tighten immigration procedures even more [142]. Germany responded with the stepped-up expropriation and concentration measures and acts of violence that marked Nazi Jewish policy in 1938–39, especially following the annexation of Austria and the occupation of the Czech lands. This unambiguous pressure to leave meant that Austrian and Czech Jews showed little of the uncertainty that German Jews displayed during the beginning of Nazi rule: some 130,000 of 185,000 Jews from Austria and 35,000 of 118,000 from Czechoslovakia fled between occupation and the outbreak of war [76; 95]. Moreover, in July 1939 the regime replaced the Reichsvertretung with a new body, the Reichsvereinigung*, whose explicit purpose was 'to further the emigration of the Jews' [2 *p. 140*].

Vigorous protests against the Nazi terror were launched in the West; after Kristallnacht the United States even recalled its ambassador to Berlin. But the German policy of brutally prodding Jews into flight effectively challenged protesting countries to relax their barriers against refugees: German propaganda chided as hypocrites those who decried persecution while denying the persecuted a haven. To counter such arguments, US President Franklin Roosevelt convened a coordinating conference of 32 potential receiving countries at Evian*, France, in July 1938. Each country was asked to explain how it could contribute to alleviating the refugee crisis; however, it was stipulated in advance that no country would be asked to change any of its existing immigration policies [86; 194].

Little came of the Evian Conference; almost all countries explained why they could do little more than they were already doing. The conference did create an Intergovernmental Committee on Refugees*, which negotiated with the Nazi regime about broadening the Haavara principle so as to allow emigrants to transfer significant assets to any destination while stimulating German exports worldwide; but war broke out before an agreement could be implemented [54]. In the meantime the confrontation between a German government bent increasingly upon forcing Jews out and countries reluctant to let them in continued. In 1939 German government agencies, together with German shipping lines, began purchasing visas wholesale from Latin American consular officials in Germany and reselling them to Jews together with steamship tickets. Sometimes, however, the issuing countries refused to honour them. In May 1939 this situation greeted 930 passengers on the S.S. *St Louis* who, holding Cuban tourist visas, tried to disembark in Havana: Cuban officials ordered them and their ship to leave. Petitions to the United States to relax its immigration laws so that the refugees could land there were ineffective. Finally, after two months of negotiations, Britain, France, Belgium, and Holland agreed to divide the passengers among them.

Historians differ in their evaluations of the potential receiving countries' responses to Nazi persecutions of Jews. Some see in the application of immigration restrictions to Jewish refugees an expression of extreme callousness towards the Jewish plight [96; 194], while others contend that the sheer size of the refugee flow overwhelmed well-meaning countries unequipped to handle it [61; 172]. A recent study has argued that the successful resettlement of 290,000 German, Austrian, and Czech Jews in 1938–39 indicates that in those years 'the international reception of Jewish refugees was ... generous' in light of most countries' policies of excluding virtually *all* immigrants [168 *p. 25*].

In the event, although the majority of German, Austrian, and Czech Jews did find refuge in other countries, that refuge was often granted begrudgingly and with considerable resistance. More important, potential receiving countries consistently made it clear that whatever special efforts they might make on behalf of several hundred thousand refugees from Nazi persecution would not be extended to the millions of Jews simultaneously being pressured to leave Poland, Romania, and other eastern European countries [142]. The German invasion of Poland in September 1939 and the extension of Nazi rule to 2 million Polish Jews thus complicated the implementation of Nazi Jewish policy immeasurably.

6   THE TRANSITION TO KILLING

The outbreak of war and the conquest of Poland made it virtually impossible for Germany to continue pushing Jews out of the territories it controlled, as it had been trying to do ever more intensely since 1938. Now the sheer number of Jews under German rule frightened potential receiving countries. Moreover, for Britain, France, and other states at war with the Third Reich, Jews from Germany, Austria, and the Czech lands (known since March 1939 as the Protectorate of Bohemia and Moravia*) were now legally enemy aliens. Thus, immediately following its declaration of war, Britain cancelled all visas granted previously to refugees seeking to leave those countries [187].

Realizing that the policy of extrusion could not continue, Germany began to think about unilaterally creating the 'Jewish reservation' that the foreign ministry, in its January 1939 policy statement, had hoped would be established by international action. This reservation would have to be located on territory Germany already controlled. Initially, thinking centred about a part of the Lublin district near the town of Nisko*, at the southeastern extreme of the Generalgouvernement. As early as October 1939, Jews from Vienna and the Protectorate were forcibly resettled in this region; transports soon followed from Germany and western Poland. By January 1940, 78,000 Jews had been moved into the area, with plans underfoot for transporting 400,000 more there shortly [95]. Following the fall of France in June 1940, German attentions turned to the French African colony of Madagascar, highly preferable to Lublin in its distance from areas where Germans might settle. This idea was connected, however, with German efforts to reach a comprehensive agreement with Britain (which controlled the sea routes to East Africa) about the disposal of all African colonies. When those efforts failed, and Germany began preparing actively for the invasion of the Soviet Union, the Madagascar reservation project was abandoned [63; 196].

Still, Germany did not immediately abandon its policy of eliminating Jews through emigration, expulsion, or deportation. During 1940 and early 1941 it continued to try to help Jews leave Reich territory. Adolf Eichmann, who had supervised the Central Offices for Jewish Emigration in Vienna and Prague and had assumed control of a similar Reich-wide agency in October 1939, actively assisted German Jews in using escape routes through Italy and Lithuania and worked with Soviet and Japanese authorities in arranging for thousands of Jews to travel via the trans-Siberian railroad to the International Settlements at Shanghai [63; 187]. He also cooperated with clandestine Jewish efforts to circumvent British restrictions on immigration to Palestine [54]. On occasion German Jews were forcibly expelled westward; 6,504 were sent to unoccupied France in October 1940, hundreds more in sealed trains to Lisbon the following month [65; 194]. In all, 15,000 Jews left Germany proper in 1940, despite wartime difficulties; tens of thousands more left other German-controlled territories.

But in the summer and autumn of 1941 German practice reversed itself. Orders given in August and October prohibited all further Jewish departures from German-occupied areas. Germany was now seeking not to drive Jews away but to keep them locked in. This reversal suggests a radical change in the Nazi regime's immediate plans for dealing with the Jews under its control. Indeed, it was precisely during the summer of 1941 that the first organized, indiscriminate mass killings of Jews took place. Such killings began shortly following Germany's invasion of the Soviet Union on 22 June 1941. Over the next five months, mobile killing squads, known as *Einsatzgruppen**, together with regular German army units, shot and killed half a million Jews on Soviet or Soviet-occupied territory [111; 178]. By November 1941 preparations were underway for the construction of special killing centres* in occupied Poland, where over 3.5 million Jews from throughout Europe would be gassed to death by late 1944. In other words, the ban on emigration coincided with the transition to active systematic mass murder.

What brought about this transition? Was it connected in any way with the diminishing returns of the policy of extrusion?

WHY BEGIN KILLING?

Predictably, there is much debate over these questions. For intentionalist historians, the adjustment was one not of policy goals but merely of method and pace. In their view, total physical annihilation of all Jews within Germany's reach had long been Hitler's aim, and all that the Nazi regime had done prior to the beginning of mass shootings and gassings had been planned to advance that end. In fact, some of them have argued that the beginnings of actual killing operations should be set not in 1941 but in 1939, when Nazi authorities began to mandate establishment of ghettos in occupied Poland.

This argument is based largely on the fact that the ghettos created throughout Poland in 1939–41 were often themselves sites of mass death. Indeed, as they were set up they could hardly have been otherwise [*Doc. 10*]. Generally they were located in poorer parts of town, where sanitary conditions were often substandard. Living space was hopelessly overcrowded: in Warsaw, for example, 450,000 Jews were crammed into 1.3 square miles, with more than seven persons for each available room. Restrictions on food supplies often left rations for Jews at around 1,000 calories, sometimes even below 200. Such conditions produced extraordinary mortality. Perhaps half a million Polish Jews died before systematic mass killing began, 43,000 of them in Warsaw during 1941 alone [104; 111]. Had the Germans merely continued the harsh ghetto regime, Polish Jewry might well have died out altogether within less than a decade. Hence, it has been claimed, the change-over from 'indirect extermination' in ghettos to active killing reflected nothing more than Nazi dissatisfaction with the pace at which Jews were perishing [84 *p. 259*].

That dissatisfaction supposedly became acute during the winter or spring of 1941, when Germany began actively planning the invasion of the Soviet Union. At that time some 4 million Jews inhabited Soviet-held territory, more than double the number already under German rule. Hitler's world-view suggested that Soviet Jews must be especially dangerous, having successfully wielded their Marxist-Bolshevik ideology to subdue the Russian nation. Thus, noting that on 13 March 1941 German Chief of Staff Wilhelm Keitel defined the impending war against the Soviets as 'the decisive struggle that will have to be carried out between ... two opposing political systems' [2 *p. 375*], and that Hitler himself told his generals two weeks later that the war against communism was to be a 'war of extermination' [5 *p. 346*], some historians contend that the decision to attack the USSR signalled that the time had come to complete the long-planned physical extirpation of the Jews [77; 115; 128]. While the campaign was being planned, they argue, Hitler gave an oral order that all Jews should be killed.

The functionalist view, in contrast, holds that systematic killing did not become a policy goal until after the invasion of the USSR had begun. Those who take this position implicitly or explicitly reject the view that ghettos were intended from the start to produce mass death among Polish Jews, noting that it is a logical fallacy to infer the goal of an action from its outcome. Christopher Browning's research on Nazi ghettoization policy has strengthened this opinion. Browning found that local Nazi officials in occupied Poland set up ghettos on their own initiative, without orders from Berlin, as what they hoped would be a temporary solution to the problems created by the delay in establishing a Jewish reservation. He also showed that in Warsaw and Łódź, the two largest ghettos, senior officials tried to prevent Jewish attrition, hoping to exploit the ghetto population's labour [65]. Thus, some historians reason, mass killing represented a totally new direction in Nazi policy; throughout the ghetto period, and even during the first months following the Soviet invasion, the leaders of the Third Reich continued to hope that Jews could be deported *en masse* to some far-off locale. According to Martin Broszat, even as late as fall 1941 Nazi leaders 'spoke only ... of deportation "to the East" ', meaning that they planned to concentrate Jews from Germany, the Protectorate, and Poland in territories they expected to conquer from the Soviet Union, probably in Siberia [66 *pp. 85–6*]. Therefore, it has been argued, even though the *Einsatzgruppen* and German soldiers murdered hundreds and thousands of Jews on Soviet-held lands between June and November 1941 and placed even more in ghettos to await later slaughter, those killings should not be viewed as part of a comprehensive programme to annihilate all of European Jewry. Instead they were the product of a measured escalation growing out of the ideological war against 'Jewish Bolshevism': initially Jewish state and communist party officials were killed; then Jewish communal leaders and intellectuals; finally ordinary men, women, and children. Until autumn, however, if not even later, the Germans had no concrete plans systematically to kill any other than Soviet Jews [148; 178].

Those plans changed, according to this thesis, only after it became clear that the anticipated German conquest of Soviet territory was not proceeding as expected. In the wake of the invasion, plans had begun to be made to make major German cities 'Jew-pure' (*judenrein*) by deporting all their Jewish inhabitants 'to the east', but those plans were thwarted by the failure of the German army to capture the necessary eastern dumping ground. Instead of changing course, however, top Nazi officials decided to send German Jews to ghettos in Poland or in occupied Soviet lands. Those ghettos were already filled to capacity, a fact that angered the local Nazi officials who had to receive the deportees. In response, local officials in certain ghettos concluded that in order to prevent intolerable overcrowding they would have either to shoot the newcomers as soon as they came or to kill some current ghetto inhabitants. Thus on 7 November 1941 a mass shooting of Minsk Jews cleared room for 1,500 Jewish deportees from Hamburg. On 25–29 November deportees from five different German cities were shot upon arrival in Kaunas; on 30 November the same fate befell 1,000 Jews deported from Berlin to Riga. These local initiatives are said to have indicated an escape from the 'blind alley into which the Nazis had manoeuvred themselves' when they deported German Jews eastward without being prepared to receive them. Hence, in Broszat's words, 'the practice of liquidation ... gained predominance and evolved ... into a comprehensive "programme" ' to murder all Jews throughout Europe [66 *p. 93*]. Some proponents of this thesis assume that Hitler ratified this development with an oral order for systematic Europe-wide mass killing in late 1941; others contend that although Hitler unquestionably approved and encouraged mass killing, he did not need to order it explicitly.

Historians' disagreements about when direct systematic murder of all Jews became the Third Reich's active official policy stem largely from a lack of clear documentation. No written order for a comprehensive killing programme, from Hitler or anyone else, has been found. Almost all scholars today believe that no such order was ever put in writing; at most there was an oral instruction 'or, more probably, a broad hint that everybody understood' [88 *p. xiii*]. But such a hint is virtually impossible to trace. Moreover, most extant documents that seem to reflect the transition to killing are maddeningly ambiguous. German officials typically employed euphemisms to avoid speaking directly about killing, to the point where, in one scholar's words, 'the best-kept, most organized files are not necessarily the key to [understanding the genesis of] ... mass murder on an unprecedented scale' [60 *p. 32*]. For example, on 31 July 1941 Hermann Goering commissioned Reinhard Heydrich 'to carry out all necessary preparations ... for a total solution of the Jewish question ... in Europe' [*Doc. 11*]. However, this order did not state explicitly that that 'total solution' (or 'final solution', a phrase also used in the document) was to involve mass killing. On the contrary, it represented itself as a 'supplement' to a January 1939 instruction 'to solve the Jewish question by emigration and evacuation'. Did the order mean that the 'final solution' was to be sought through 'emigration and evacuation' (perhaps to Siberia, which in July 1941 the Germans still thought they would soon conquer)? In earlier Nazi documents the phrase had been used in this sense. Or did it mean that a new 'final solution' was now to replace 'emigration and evacuation'? There is no way to be certain.

The volume of such tantalizing but imprecise documents is enormous. Moreover, new documentary discoveries take place regularly. With more and more evidence brought into the historiographical debate, historians have recently staked out a range of positions between the intentionalist and functionalist poles. Browning, for example, while affirming the functionalist dating of the decision to begin mass killing on a continental scale to autumn 1941, has rejected the local initiative argument, ascribing the impetus for the decision primarily to Hitler and suggesting that the possibility of mass murder had been on the dictator's mind even earlier in the year [65]. Philippe Burrin, describing himself as a 'conditional intentionalist', has claimed that Hitler had long regarded either extrusion or killing as acceptable approaches to dealing with Jews, although he decided firmly upon killing only in autumn 1941 [70]. On the other hand, Richard Breitman, while accepting the intentionalist position that the decision was taken by Hitler in early 1941 in conjunction with the planning of the Soviet invasion, has contended that the Nazi leader did not even entertain the thought of mass killing until the eve of war, much less systematically lay the groundwork for it from the moment he came to power [60]. The three scholars disagree over what sparked the decision: for Browning it was euphoria over the initial victories against the Soviets, for Burrin anxiety over Germany's military position once the Soviet invasion had stalled, and for Breitman the realization that a world conflagration, in which both the USSR and the United States would join Britain against the Axis, was about to begin.

Still other historians have tried to reconceptualize the issue altogether by connecting the decision to kill Jews to broader goals and policies of the Third Reich. Studies by Michael Burleigh, Wolfgang Wippermann, and Henry Friedlander have argued that Jews were murdered as part of a general programme to create a German racial utopia, in which all who threatened the Nazi vision of an ideal 'Aryan Germanic race' – not only Jews, but Sinti and Roma, the handicapped, and (for Burleigh and Wippermann) the so-called 'asocials'* (habitual criminals and derelicts) and homosexuals – were deemed 'life unworthy of life' and condemned to eventual death [69; 89]. Noting that many techniques employed in the mass murder of Jews after 1942 were tried out on a smaller scale against the handicapped by the so-called T4 organization* in 1939–40 and that T4 personnel were later heavily involved in slaughtering Jews and Gypsies, Friedlander argued that 'one cannot explain any one of these Nazi killing operations without explaining the others' [89 *p. 295*]. Thus, he implied, the anti-Jewish murder campaign had always been intended, and the timing of its onset depended less upon circumstances surrounding the invasion of the Soviet Union and the failure of the extrusion policy than upon the success of T4 in perfecting methods that could be used against larger population groups as well.

Similarly, Götz Aly and Susanne Heim have maintained that the Holocaust can be understood only against the background of Nazi Germany's overall economic and population policies in eastern Europe. In their view, the Nazis hoped to colonize millions of Germans in the conquered eastern territories but saw overpopulation in those areas as a primary impediment to achieving this goal. Killing off large segments of the local population, including certain categories of Slavs as well as Jews, was supposed to overcome this problem, thereby stimulating economic modernization in a backward part of the world. According to Aly and Heim, this idea was formulated around 1938–39 by a group of young social scientists working for the Nazi regime and made such good sense to policy-makers that it was implemented during the occupation of Poland. Echoing the intentionalist position and in opposition to Browning, they believe that ghettos and Jewish reservations were indeed meant to serve as instruments of mass death by starvation, with active killing beginning once it became clear that the ghettos represented a severe economic burden. Unlike intentionalists, however, they claim that it was not any particular animus towards Jews but cold-hearted, rational economic thinking that underlay the intention of mass murder [38; 108].

The Aly–Heim thesis attracted much critical comment, and most historians have rejected it [43; 78; 110]. In general the historiographical mainstream continues to separate the killing of Jews analytically from Nazi persecutions of other groups, believing that fundamentally different sets of considerations were at work in each case. Nonetheless, historians' views are constantly changing as new documents are brought to light and analysed from different perspectives. The question of why the Third Reich began actively and systematically to murder the Jews of Europe in 1941 is far from settled.

THE MEANS OF MURDER

In any event, it is clear that by the end of 1941 the phrase 'final solution' stood for mass murder. On 29 November Heydrich invited representatives of thirteen government, party, and police agencies to a conference, 'followed by luncheon', to discuss 'the remaining work connected with this final solution' [*Doc. 12*]. The meeting, known as the Wannsee conference* (after the address where it was held), was set for 9 December, then postponed to 20 January 1942. According to the conference minutes, Heydrich noted that 'emigration has now been replaced by evacuation of the Jews to the east, as a further possible solution, with the appropriate prior authorization by the Führer'.

'Evacuation' was, to be sure, only 'a provisional option', Heydrich explained, 'but it is already supplying practical experience of great significance in view of the coming final solution of the Jewish question' [2 p. 253]. As part of that 'coming final solution', young, healthy Jews would be sent to forced labour, 'during which a large proportion will no doubt drop out through natural reduction'. The surviving remnant would 'require suitable treatment', for it would represent a physically resistant strain 'that could, on its release, become the germ cell of a new Jewish revival' [2 p. 256]. Virtually all historians agree that, in this context, 'suitable treatment' meant killing. Indeed, as preparations for the Wannsee conference were being made, construction of six special centres for mass killing – Chełmno*, Bełżec*, Sobibór*, Treblinka*, Majdanek*, and Birkenau* (Auschwitz II) – was already underway. In these centres some 60 per cent of Jewish victims were to meet their deaths [188].

Building the killing centres signalled a change in German methods of murdering Jews. Jews in Soviet-held lands had been killed mainly by shooting: units of the *Einsatzgruppen*, police, or regular army would enter a town, seize some or all of its Jews, march them to a secluded location in a nearby forest, force the Jews to dig a pit, line them up at the pit's edge, and shoot them one by one in the back of the head [Doc. 13]. In 1941–42 some 1.4 million Jews from the USSR, Lithuania, Latvia, Estonia, and eastern Poland were murdered in this fashion. This method, however, had several disadvantages. It was slow and often incomplete: for example, although shooting squads killed over 33,000 Jews in Kiev in late September 1941, another 120,000 remained in the city after this operation. Shooting also required considerable manpower, which was not easily spared from battlefield duty; eventually personnel had to be drawn not only from German forces but from native collaborators, whose number approached 300,000 by the end of 1942 [65]. Involvement of such large numbers made it difficult to keep the killing operations secret – a difficulty that, it was feared, could lead to unrest among the conquered non-Jewish populations, who were liable to wonder whether they might become the conquerors' next targets. And mass shootings generated undesirable psychological repercussions in some German executioners, who found the messy business of shooting – the screaming, the blood, the stench, and (perhaps most of all) the direct confrontation with their victims – emotionally devastating. Some killing squads reported problems with alcoholism; nervous breakdowns, albeit infrequent, were noted. A German commander grumbled after a shooting that his men were now 'finished for the rest of their lives'. 'What kind of followers are we training here?', he complained, 'either neurotics or savages!' [111, 1 *p. 332*]. Thus, for the murder of all European Jews, a method was required that could kill greater numbers faster, require less manpower, be kept hidden from the local population, and maximize the psychological distance between killer and killed.

Killing centres satisfied these requirements. They promised efficiency: instead of sending the killers after Jews, who were spread over a wide area, Jews from all over Europe would be brought to specially constructed central locations, which, by consolidating operations and processing the victims in assembly-line fashion, would demand the involvement of far fewer Germans than had mass shooting. In fact, the process could be designed so as to permit use of a relatively small number of non-German collaborators, and even some Jews, to perform the most gruesome tasks associated with the actual killing and subsequent disposal of corpses, thereby sparing Germans the emotional strain of having to confront the results of their actions directly. Reducing the number of personnel involved and locating the centres in areas under direct German control also increased the chances of maintaining secrecy. Thus at Wannsee it was decided that 'Europe is to be combed through from west to east', with Jews 'taken group by group to ... transit ghettos, in order to be transported further east from there' [2 *p. 256*]. 'East' in this case meant Poland, where the six killing centres began operations between December 1941 and July 1942.

The centres killed their victims by asphyxiation. At Chełmno, the first to begin operation, Jews were loaded onto sealed vans whose exhaust fumes were channelled back into the cargo area. At Bełżec, Sobibór, Treblinka, and Majdanek, diesel engines sent carbon monoxide into specially constructed gas chambers, while at Birkenau the chambers employed the more efficient hydrogen cyanide, marketed under the trade name Zyklon B*.

Sometimes the killing centres are called 'concentration camps', but this is a misnomer. Nazi Germany did erect many concentration camps – Dachau, Sachsenhausen, Buchenwald, and Mauthausen are among the most infamous – for incarcerating political prisoners and 'asocials', but they were not employed in the mass killing of Jews [160]. To be sure, Majdanek housed both a concentration camp and a killing centre, and Birkenau was situated next to the concentration camp at Auschwitz. Jews brought to these locations underwent 'selection'*: those thought fit for labour were sent to the camp, while the others were killed immediately. Also at Birkenau several thousand Jews were chosen as subjects for medical experiments between 1942 and 1944. At the four remaining killing centres, however, Jews were killed upon arrival, except for the few chosen for the *Sonderkommando** (special command), whose job was to press the victims into the gas chambers and transport their corpses for incineration or burial [*Doc. 14*]. There was also a network of forced labour camps*, including Płaszów, Janowska, and Trawniki, in which as many as half a million Jews (mostly from Poland) were incarcerated and where exhausted workers were often killed on the spot [87].

ORGANIZING THE TRANSPORTS

With the killing centres established, the Germans faced the task of bringing millions of Jews from throughout Europe to them. That presented a logistical challenge of the first order. Transports of Jews had to be scheduled so that killing installations would be neither overloaded nor idle. Railroad tracks had to be cleared; cars, locomotives, and personnel had to be allocated. Round-ups of Jews needed to be coordinated with local military and civilian authorities. The agency that oversaw these operations was the SS*. Led by Heinrich Himmler, the SS controlled all police functions in the Reich, including surveillance and repression of those deemed threats on ideological or racial grounds. This aspect of SS work, which encompassed Jewish matters, was supervised by Heydrich, head of the internal intelligence and secret police service, the Reich Main Security Office (RSHA*). Heydrich, in consultation with Himmler, in turn assigned responsibility for direct administration of the murder scheme to Adolf Eichmann.

At Wannsee Eichmann had received the general instruction to 'comb Europe from west to east'. That guideline, though, proved difficult to follow. At the time, the westernmost country from which Jews were to be deported, France, with 350,000 Jews, was technically self-governing; Germany, needing to concentrate its manpower on the Soviet and African fronts, was thus heavily dependent upon French police and administrators to identify, concentrate, and hand over potential deportees. Similar situations prevailed in Denmark and Norway. Non-German officials also retained influence in Belgium and, to a lesser extent, Holland. Italy and Finland were independent German allies that would have to be cajoled into cooperating in the murder programme. Such was the case too with Germany's allies to the south-east – Slovakia, Hungary, Croatia, Romania, and Bulgaria – while most of Greece was under Italian occupation. In contrast, Germany had virtually complete control over the Jews in Austria, the Protectorate, Poland, the Baltic states, the occupied Soviet areas, and Serbia, as well as Germany proper. Except for Serbia (where most Jewish men had already been shot between August and December 1941 in reprisal for the Serbian communist partisan revolt that followed the invasion of the USSR), these were the countries closest to the killing centres; deporting Jews from them thus presented the fewest logistical difficulties. Besides, they contained three-quarters of the Reich's intended victims. Small wonder that Jews from these countries became the first casualties of the continent-wide murder campaign, or that the percentage losses of their Jewish communities were, with few exceptions, greater than those elsewhere. Although as early as March 1942 tens of thousands of Jews were deported from France and Slovakia, the Germans placed primary emphasis in the year after Wannsee on making the countries under their direct control totally free of Jews.

The most elaborate such effort, to make the entire Generalgouvernement of Poland *judenrein*, was known as Operation Reinhard* (after Heydrich). Under the direction of Odilo Globocnik*, SS commander in Lublin and a confidant of Himmler, planning for it began even before the Wannsee conference. Globocnik and his staff designed both the gassing installations at Bełżec, Sobibór, and Treblinka and the process for bringing Polish Jews to them. Between March 1942 and October 1943 that process resulted in the liquidation of ghettos in Lublin, Warsaw, Lwów, Kraków, Częstochowa, Białsystok, and hundreds of smaller towns and the death of over 2 million Jews [39]. In all ghettos the process (known as an *Aktion**) was similar. The day before the scheduled deportation, posters instructed ghetto residents to report for 'resettlement in the east'*. The next day Germans and non-German collaborators sealed off the ghetto exits. If not enough Jews reported, searches were conducted from house to house. Those caught in the search were brought forcibly to a railroad siding, where they were packed into freight cars and shipped to a killing centre [*Doc. 15*]. Sometimes these *Aktionen* lasted for months, as in Lublin, where 33,000 Jews were sent to Bełżec between 17 March and 20 April, or in Warsaw, where 265,000 were transported to Treblinka between 22 July and 12 September. Sometimes the pace of deportation was so great that not enough railroad cars were available; in those cases police units were despatched to kill small-town Jews by shooting [64].

For all of the brutality of the *Aktionen*, the Germans appear to have hoped that Jews would board the deportation trains voluntarily.

To this end they engaged in elaborate tactics of deception. By presenting the deportations as 'resettlement', and by instructing the deportees to take baggage with them, they tried to persuade Jews that they would be moved to areas where there was plenty of room to live. Jews were told that they were important to the German war effort, that in their new homes they would be put to work, and that they would have adequate food and shelter so that they could be most productive. 'Resettlement', in other words, was made to appear as a desirable alternative to the crowding, hunger, and disease of the ghettos. At the same time the Germans tried to weaken Jews' will to resist, both by acting with speed and surprise and by setting different segments of Jewish society against one another. Declaring certain categories of people immune from deportation encouraged Jews to compete with one another over the limited number of exemptions. Jews striving to obtain exemptions for themselves would be less inclined to demonstrate solidarity with the entire community, a prerequisite for effective resistance. Undermining solidarity was achieved also by compelling Jewish administrators in the ghettos to post the deportation orders and holding them responsible for supplying a daily quota of deportees. Indeed, ghetto administrators often found themselves in the position of selecting the deportees and using Jewish police squads (which the Germans had established in many ghettos for maintaining internal order) to force recalcitrant designees to the trains.

Such tactics pointed to a German understanding that, even in the territories under complete Nazi control, the ability to realize the 'final solution' depended partly upon German success in manoeuvring the designated victims into the most favourable position for taking their lives. In this sense, the architects of the murder campaign regarded the victims' behaviour as critical to its outcome: victims who perceived a mortal threat might theoretically have taken action to avoid it, and those with the ability might have tried to foil it. Similarly, they realized that bystanders – local non-Jewish populations, underground resistance movements, governments of countries fighting Germany, even people outside the Nazi orbit – might influence the results of their crusade. In theory, under certain circumstances bystanders could provide information to potential victims that could help them evaluate their situation accurately, or they could even help victims escape or defeat the threat. Hence the job of organizing the transports to the killing centres necessarily involved careful consideration of the reactions of victims and bystanders to the German machinations.

7 RESPONDING TO MURDER

Though the Nazis evidently believed that victims' and bystanders' behaviour might affect the eventual success of their murder campaign, it is a matter of considerable controversy whether their belief was well founded. Ever since the German defeat, scholars and non-scholars have debated intensely, often bitterly, whether Jews or anyone else, within the Nazi orbit or outside it, could have done anything that would have significantly altered the outcome of the murder programme once it was launched. Ultimately, of course, the question cannot be answered with any confidence: what might have happened if actions not taken had been taken is a matter for speculation, nothing more. Historians can, however, ascertain fairly reliably what sort of options were available to various categories of victims and bystanders in responding to the onset and progress of mass murder and record the choices different groups made as the campaign unfolded. They can also explore the reasons why certain responses were exhibited and others not.

INFORMATION AND IMAGINATION

In doing so, scholars and non-scholars must be aware that they observe the victims' and bystanders' actions with the benefit of hindsight. As historian Yehuda Bauer has noted, 'The post-Holocaust generation ... already know[s] ... that mass murder was possible; [Jews and non-Jews] who lived at the time did not. For them it was a totally new reality that was unfolding before their shocked eyes and paralyzed minds' [53 p. 7]. The extent of that mental paralysis was revealed starkly in July 1943, when Jan Karski*, a Polish underground courier who had witnessed the killing of Jews in a labour camp, met with senior advisers to Franklin Roosevelt and related what he had seen. One of the advisers, Supreme Court Justice Felix Frankfurter (himself a Jew and ardent Zionist), reportedly responded

that he was 'unable to believe' Karski's eyewitness testimony. Not
that he doubted the truth of what he had heard: as Frankfurter is supposed to have explained, 'I did not say that this young man is lying; I
said that I am unable to believe him. There is a difference' [192
p. 188]. The inability to believe stories of behaviour seemingly incon-
gruous with the image of modern civilized humanity was to retard the
reactions of many who confronted the mounting holocaust.

Moreover, like German Jews following Hitler's accession to
power, victims and bystanders throughout Europe had no direct
access to German discussions of the murder campaign. They had to
assess Nazi designs on the basis of indirect signals that were often
vague, contradictory, and misleading. Such was the case both before
and after systematic killing had begun. Different agencies of the Nazi
regime often seemed to disagree about how Jews should be treated –
as indeed they frequently did. Following the invasion of Poland, for
example, when SS units had undertaken considerable gratuitous
violence against Jews and Poles (hoping to terrorize the conquered
population into submission), the German army command, believing
that terror generated panic instead of order and made the job of controlling the civilian population more difficult, had voiced strong
objections, even placing some perpetrators of violence on trial. Governor General Frank opposed the Nisko reservation project and interfered with the resettlement of Jews from outside the Generalgouvernement; as a result, resettlement transports were sometimes halted
on route and returned to their point of origin. Ghettos were not
formed according to a uniform schedule but at an uneven pace (and in
some towns not at all); sometimes (as in Warsaw) there were false
starts before ghettos were finally sealed.

Inferring any consistent policy from such inconsistent behaviour
was difficult at best, even if a consistent policy had been formulated
behind the scenes. If anything, Nazi actions in occupied Poland and
elsewhere initially appeared to sophisticated Jewish and non-Jewish
observers to be aimed at plundering Jewish wealth, providing a psychological outlet for Germans convinced of their own racial superior-
ity, and exploiting local antipathy towards Jews to endear the conquerors to the conquered, but not necessarily at implementing any
single preconceived idea about how the so-called Jewish question
ought to be solved [*Doc. 16*]. In an eyewitness report from March
1940 on conditions for Polish Jews under German occupation, for
example, Moshe Kleinbaum, a leading Jewish journalist and political
figure, spoke of the 'arbitrariness and treachery of the Nazi authorities', meaning that the regime was characterized by 'awful corruption'

and that 'in exchange for gold everything can be gotten', including freedom from persecution [9 *p. 278*]. That was an assessment based upon dozens of testimonies that Kleinbaum had gathered from Jews and non-Jews who related to him their actual day-to-day experiences with the occupiers – seemingly more reliable indicators of the future than Hitler's rantings in *Mein Kampf* or the rhetorical bombasts of Nazi politicians in Berlin. Mass killing contradicted those experiences and suggested that previous assessments of Nazi policy were no longer valid. Thus it necessitated a mental readjustment that was not easy to achieve.

Hence, when in the summer and autumn of 1941 the occasional survivors of mass shootings in former Soviet territories began to relate their stories to anyone who would listen, they were often dismissed [*Doc. 17*]. Only after such stories were heard again and again could the natural and experiential resistance to believing them be overcome. Even then, it required both the collation of data from many different places and a radical leap of imagination to deduce that all Jews throughout Europe, and not merely some on the extreme eastern frontier of the Nazi orbit, were slated for death, no matter where they lived, what acts they had committed, or how much gold they could offer to annul the sentence [132]. Collating the necessary data was impeded by the German determination to camouflage the murder campaign, by strict German control over information sources, and by the barriers the ghetto walls presented to communication, both between Jews and non-Jews and among the ghettos themselves. Imagination in the necessary degree was by nature the possession of only a gifted few.

Perhaps, then, it was no accident that the first person to deduce that the Germans had decided to murder each and every Jew within their reach (or at least the first person to articulate such a deduction) was a young poet and Zionist youth movement leader from Wilno, Abba Kovner*, who in late December 1941 announced to his movement comrades that 'a total system' existed for 'the annihilation of millions' of Jews [*Doc. 18*]. Jewish youth movement members had several advantages in overcoming the information blackout and isolation of the ghettos. Youth movements, a widespread feature of Jewish life in interwar Poland, were organized on a countrywide basis, so that members from different cities maintained regular contact with one another. They trained their members, usually in their teens or early twenties, to see themselves as part of an *avant-garde*, thereby reinforcing normal youthful adventurousness and daring. Many members had excellent command of the Polish language, which enabled them to pass as Poles when the need arose. These characteristics helped youth movements serve as primary vehicles for clandestine inter-ghetto communication. Nonetheless, Kovner's perception was initially exceptional even among youth movement members; indeed, once he made his announcement, some comrades questioned how he could be so certain. Kovner confessed that his deduction came mainly from 'a healthy instinct'; it was evidently his poet's sensibility, not any particular information, that brought him to it. Yet even that poet's sensibility did not produce his conclusion until almost six months after the first mass killings in his own town had taken place. How much more difficult would it be for less exceptional individuals, farther removed from the initial killing sites and facing ever greater German efforts at deception, to follow him.

Kovner made his deduction on the basis of information about mass shootings alone. Stories about killing centres began to filter back into the ghettos of the Generalgouvernement shortly after the centres went into operation. By April 1942 a clandestine Jewish documentation unit in Warsaw, led by the historian and activist Emmanuel Ringelblum* for the purpose of collecting and distributing information about the condition of Polish Jewry under German rule and the ways in which Jews were coping with occupation, had learned of the killing centres in Chełmno and Bełżec and understood that the Lublin Jews recently deported had been sent to their deaths [132]. The next month the leadership of the underground Jewish socialist party, the Bund*, concluded that the Germans had formulated a plan to kill all the Jews of Poland. It incorporated that assessment into a comprehensive report on Polish Jewry, which it delivered through Polish underground channels to the Polish government-in-exile in London [*Doc. 19*]. This report constituted the first detailed statement about killing centres received in the West and the first document to suggest that a programme to murder all Polish Jews was being implemented [80].

The Bund report, however, represented only the first stage in the gradual unfolding of Jewish awareness of Nazi designs. It demonstrated that segments of the Jewish political leadership in Poland understood the danger that faced their community, but it did not prove that all members of the community shared their appraisal. Little research has been done on how ordinary Polish Jews perceived their situation, and that research has been inconclusive [83]. Moreover, the Bund's evaluation emphasized Poland, not other European countries. Jews in western, central, and southeastern Europe, far removed from the killing centres, had to gather information on their own concerning the fate of their brethren deported to Poland and to derive the appropriate inference themselves, in the face of Nazi deception efforts and their own psychological indisposition to do so. Many, especially in western Europe, thought that even if stories of mass killing of Polish and Soviet Jews were true, their own fate would surely be different, because of their supposedly higher cultural level and their greater degree of integration into the surrounding society. In the end, it appears that only a relatively small number understood that 'resettlement to the east' almost invariably meant death. Postwar testimonies of the proportionately few survivors of deportations from France, Holland, Greece, Hungary, and other Nazi-dominated countries outside Poland indicate that many had no idea where they were going until they arrived [132].

In other words, the choices Jews made in responding to Nazi domination were not always informed ones.

COMMUNAL RESPONSIBILITY AND STRATEGIES FOR SURVIVAL

Generally, those best able to assess Nazi intentions were associated with groups that took responsibility for Jewish communities. Yet even among those who could make informed choices there was much diversity of response to the German threat once it became clear.

In most occupied countries the Germans imposed an official governing body upon the Jewish population, charging it with registering Jews and Jewish property, enforcing German directives, and maintaining health, welfare, and order among the Jewish population. In western Europe these were usually countrywide organizations, like the Reichsvereinigung in Germany, the Joodse Raad (Jewish Council) in Holland, the Union Générale des Israélites de France, or the Association des Juifs en Belgique. In Poland and the former Soviet-held territories, in contrast, each ghetto had its own 'Jewish council' or 'Council of Elders' (*Judenrat* or *Ältestenrat*), with no superior body to coordinate among them. The imposed Jewish administrations, which were in closer contact with the German authorities than other segments of Jewish society, were often among the first to pierce the Nazi veil of deception. Theoretically they were thus in a powerful position to influence their fellow Jews' behaviour in the face of the German murder programme. In practice, however, the degree and manner of their influence varied.

Understanding the responses of the official Jewish administrations to mass killing depends upon recognizing that, except in the former

Soviet-held territories, they were established before systematic murder began. Consequently, prior to the onset of deportations to the killing centres, each had already developed a relationship with the occupiers. For the most part that relationship was predicated on the assumption that Germany would sooner or later be defeated, as it had been in the First World War. This was a comforting thought. So too was the prevailing perception that the occupiers were interested primarily in extracting as much wealth from Jews as possible, for if this was the case, then the Germans were treating Jews rationally as an economic resource and could be negotiated with on a rational basis. From these premises it followed that Jews needed primarily to buy time, to do what they could to cultivate the Germans' favour sufficiently to guarantee themselves the minimum conditions required for day-to-day survival and to forestall the execution of any long-range evil Nazi designs. The sensible thing to do was to give the Germans whatever they requested – usually money, property, or labour service – as long as it was possible to do so. Resistance to German demands would be counter-productive, as it might anger the occupiers to the point where they would cease to deal with the Jews rationally and begin to give violent expression to their hostile emotions. On the other hand, cooperation might inspire German confidence in the Jewish administration, which could perhaps be exploited at crucial points in order to improve day-to-day conditions of Jewish life [184].

An early example of such thinking in action came from Warsaw. In October 1939 German press gangs began kidnapping Jewish passersby for forced labour details, making Jews fear to leave their homes. Their lives disrupted to the point of paralysis, some Jews turned to the recently established *Judenrat* in the hope that it could persuade the authorities to mitigate the terror the kidnappings had sown. Led by chairman Adam Czerniaków*, the *Judenrat* proposed to take upon itself the responsibility of supplying the occupiers with labourers if the Germans would stop the random abductions. The authorities agreed. From that time the *Judenrat* conscripted a regular labour battalion, although kidnapping did not cease entirely [*Doc. 20*].

This episode illustrated the equivocal position in which the official Jewish administrations stood as intermediaries between the German occupiers and Jewish communities. In its effort to ameliorate Jewish hardship, the Warsaw *Judenrat* had voluntarily undertaken to cater to German desires. It had also assumed the role of selecting the Jews to be delivered to the Germans for forced labour and compelling them to serve. In this way, as the initial impetus to its intervention was gradually forgotten, the *Judenrat* increasingly appeared to Warsaw

Jews more as an instrument of German oppression than as a body fighting for Jewish interests [104]. Yet the regulation of forced labour was actually one of the Warsaw *Judenrat's* most notable successes. More often its interventions on the Jews' behalf were for naught; and, as Czerniaków noted in his diary, 'when my efforts fail ... [the Jews] blame me ... as if the outcome had depended on me' [13 *p. 172*]. Indeed, not only in Warsaw but in every Jewish community administered by a German-imposed governing body, the appointed community heads had virtually no leverage with the occupiers except bribery, which they had increasingly to finance with levies upon their charges. The Germans meant them to be their functionaries, often holding them personally responsible for the behaviour of their communities. Ironically, therefore, without making their communities serve German interests in some way, often against their will, they could not hope to win meaningful improvements for them.

Once mass killing began, the only meaningful improvement to be won was suspension of shooting or deportation. Some administrators who sensed the German intention – Efraim Barash* in Białystok, Moshe Merin* in Upper Silesia, M.H. Rumkowski* in Łódź, Jakob Gens* in Wilno – thought this goal could be achieved by demonstrating their communities' productive capacities: the Germans, thinking rationally, would not destroy a resource that contributed to their economy and war effort [*Doc. 21*]. There was logic to this approach; indeed, the places where it was tried generally held on longer than those where it was not. Some 70,000 Jews actually remained in the Łódź ghetto as late as August 1944, with the advancing Soviet army only 120 km away. However, because the murder programme was ultimately driven by ideology instead of rational calculation of interest, the strategy could hope at most only to achieve delay. Moreover, it carried a terrible price. It meant using the power of the Jewish administration to cajole or even force Jews to labour long and hard to meet oppressive German production demands. It also meant that Jewish administrators had to be prepared to forsake ill and elderly Jews who did not enhance production. In Łódź in September 1942 the head of the ghetto, Rumkowski, even responded to a German order to supply 20,000 Jews for deportation by handing over children under 10, arguing that it was necessary to 'cut off limbs to save the body itself' [*Doc. 22*]. Inducing Jews to accept such bitter toil and sacrifice required, among other things, convincing them that the Germans did not intend to kill them all, that deportations were meant merely to satisfy capricious cruelty, and that deportees were not necessarily murdered. Jewish administrators who adopted the 'salvation through work'* approach thus tended to pass on to their communities only calming assessments of German intentions. Some even suppressed information that might have led to a more pessimistic conclusion. Other ghetto administrations – Lublin and Warsaw are notable examples – appear to have had no strategy at all for confronting deportation. Indeed, the Jewish leaders in those ghettos seem to have been caught unawares when the liquidation of their communities began; they themselves tended to dismiss information that might have led to an accurate appraisal of the threat that faced them. In his diary entries for 16–22 July 1942, the week before the deportations from Warsaw began, Czerniaków spoke about rumours of impending doom sweeping the ghetto; he tried to rebut them. When he was finally commanded to post a deportation order, he responded by taking his own life [13]. Although by doing so he may have drawn a personal moral line, he also did not share his perception of threat with the ghetto population. Some ghetto residents later criticized his action for leaving them leaderless in a time of crisis [*Doc. 23*].

Indeed, in only a few cases, such as Kaunas and Minsk, were ghetto administrators a source of reliable evaluations about the fate in store for their communities. And even there, that intelligence was passed on not directly but through the intermediary of a parallel, unofficial leadership.

THE UNOFFICIAL COMMUNITY AND RESISTANCE

The fundamental predicament of the official Jewish administrations as German-controlled bodies and the tension inherent in their relations with their communities frequently prompted the establishment of voluntary communal institutions not beholden to the Germans in any way. Before the onset of mass killing such institutions played prominent roles in the Jews' daily struggle against poverty, starvation, disease, and hopelessness. Self-help organizations ran public kitchens, children's centres, refugee asylums, and medical clinics. Theatre groups, libraries, culture clubs, and music societies tried to raise the spirits of the oppressed.

Many such activities had to be undertaken surreptitiously, for the Germans effectively outlawed most unofficial Jewish public activity. Thus schools and synagogues functioned underground; newspapers were published and distributed in secret. Where food rations were at starvation levels, clandestine smuggling operations sprang up. All such activity represented a form of resistance in that it actively combated the deleterious effects of Nazi policies. But as such it also stood to compromise the official administrations, which could not allow the German authorities to perceive them as unwilling or unable to implement their designs [*Doc. 24*].

Hence voluntary institutions bred an alternative leadership. Often that leadership was provided by youth movements. In addition to their advantages in gathering and analysing information about Nazi plans, youth movements were well suited in other ways to perform this role. They inculcated in their members a powerful sense of mutual attachment and commitment, often taking on the role of surrogate families. Each movement thus created its own self-help apparatus to look after its members' welfare. The energy and skill that youth leaders brought to their task made their movements among the most effective sources of material and psychological support. In consequence, non-movement members soon gravitated towards them, to the point where the movements found themselves assuming increasing responsibility for their communities as a whole [105].

In a few places official administrations realized that by themselves they could not provide their charges with the physical and spiritual sustenance they required; thus they covertly assisted the alternative leadership or at least did not interfere with its operation. In these locations – again, most notably, Kaunas and Minsk – *Judenrat* heads shared information about Nazi designs with underground groups, thereby helping make their communities more aware of the threat they faced. More often, however, official and alternative leaders clashed with one another to a greater or lesser degree. Such clashes became especially acute once mass killing began. Although both leadership groups were among the first to grasp that every Jew had been placed under a death sentence, the youth movements usually drew operative conclusions radically different from those of the official administrators. Kovner's assessment that there was no escape from the death sentence and that flight and rescue were illusions led him to reject the 'salvation through work' approach of the head of the Wilno ghetto, Gens, in favour of a call to armed resistance [*Doc. 18*]. Despite some initial hesitation, other youth movement leaders eventually agreed: Between 1942 and 1944 Jewish armed resistance units were established in well over 100 ghettos in the Generalgouvernement, Lithuania, and former Soviet territories [52; 126].

The call to armed resistance represented a dramatic change in the strategy of the unofficial leadership, for it was not aimed primarily at survival. The heads of the Jewish fighting organizations had no illusions of forcing the Germans to abandon their murder programme, nor did they believe that taking up arms would save many Jewish lives. On the contrary, many hesitated out of fear that armed anti-German actions would invite mass reprisals – as indeed they sometimes did. Thus they adopted this path only after they were convinced that death for all Jews was certain; they saw armed resistance merely as a way to choose how they would die. Their own heroic deaths in battle would, they believed, strike a blow for the honour of the Jewish people in the face of Nazi efforts to rob Jews of their humanity; they would cause Jews to be remembered not as pathetic victims but as proud defenders of their collective integrity. As Dolek Liebeskind, leader of an underground fighting organization in the Kraków ghetto, explained in November 1942, 'We are fighting for three lines in history. For this our youth has fought and not gone like sheep to the slaughter. For this it is worthwhile even to die' [159 p. 163].

That message proved psychologically impossible for most Jews to accept; it meant giving up all hope of escaping the occupiers or outlasting them. Moreover, armed resistance was inherently an option open only to those in the ghettos physically fit for it, a number already reduced sharply by the regime of hunger and disease. And, because of a chronic scarcity of weapons, even many potential participants could not take part in actual fighting. For these reasons armed resistance never became a mass phenomenon. Nevertheless, in April 1943 the Jewish Fighting Organization* in the Warsaw ghetto engaged German forces in battle for nineteen days before the ghetto was destroyed; at the time this was the largest military action undertaken by any conquered European population, Jewish or non-Jewish [104]. Smaller-scale acts of confrontation, sabotage, or reprisal occurred in dozens of other ghettos. Similar actions were carried out by Jewish military organizations in France and Belgium, and a number of Jews in most European countries were active in general armed resistance movements. Jews fought with partisan units in most countries where such groups existed, and in Poland, the Baltic countries, and the occupied Soviet territories some specifically Jewish partisan units were formed.

In the end, though, Jews throughout Nazi-occupied Europe had virtually no realistic options for inducing the Germans to abandon their murder programme through their own actions. Individual Jews might hide or disguise themselves as non-Jews, but only with enormous difficulty; and they were almost always dependent upon non-Jewish assistance in finding shelter, obtaining food, and avoiding betrayal [Doc. 25]. Similarly, rescue or protection on a mass scale required significant non-Jewish action.

LOCAL NON-JEWISH LEADERS AND POPULATIONS: OPPOSITION AND COMPLICITY

That non-Jews, especially local non-Jewish leaders, could make a vital difference was demonstrated most graphically by the dramatic rescue of Danish Jewry in October 1943. In the face of intelligence concerning an impending deportation, Danes – spurred by clergymen and social democratic activists – spontaneously warned Copenhagen's 8,000 Jews and helped them find hiding places. As a result, during a raid on 1–2 October fewer than 300 Jews were caught. Danish underground units subsequently arranged to ferry the hiding Jews to neutral Sweden. In the end, fewer than 2 per cent of Danish Jewry perished in the Holocaust. No other occupied Jewish community had such a high survival rate [197].

There were six other countries where the majority of Jews survived the war – Belgium, Bulgaria, Finland, France, Italy, and Norway. In each the Germans encountered effective local opposition, in one form or another, to at least some facets of their deportation plans, though all but Finland had previously enacted Nazi-style anti-Jewish restrictions. Except in Norway, native governments or officials played a role in disrupting the plans made at Wannsee. Finland refused categorically to initiate any anti-Jewish actions except handing over eight refugees to the Germans [164]. The Belgian civil service interfered with the execution of measures for identifying Jews; the underground warned of scheduled round-ups and conducted reprisals against Belgians who assisted in deportation efforts (even going so far as to assassinate the official of the Jewish administration who had been posting deportation orders) [85]. As long as they were able, the Italian authorities prevented German forces stationed on their territory from taking control of local Jews, while Italian soldiers occupying parts of France, Greece, and Yugoslavia actively aided Jews seeking refuge [147; 198]. The Vichy French government, though it showed little compunction about despatching the many non-French Jewish refugees in the country to the killing centres, drew the line at deporting Jews who were French citizens [143]. In Bulgaria, vigorous protests from church leaders and intellectuals led the King and his government to defy German demands to deport Jews (although they permitted the extradition of almost all Jews from Thrace and Macedonia, formerly Greek and Yugoslav territories that Germany had helped Bulgaria to annex) [49; 71]. Similar protests by church leaders in Norway did not dissuade the Norwegian puppet government from initiating deportations, but the underground helped over half of Norway's Jews escape to Sweden [35].

Total or partial opposition to the German murder programme was facilitated in these countries by the relative freedom of action enjoyed in them by local officials. Yet, as the case of Norway shows, relative local autonomy did not guarantee protection in high places. In fact, in two Nazi satellite states, Slovakia and Croatia, the native governments actually precipitated deportations on their own. Slovak authorities consistently pressed the Germans to remove Jews from the country, even offering to pay for each Jew sent away. In Croatia much actual killing was done by the *Ustaše**, a state-sponsored militia, which not only perpetrated pogroms with shocking brutality but erected special camps where incarcerated Jews (and Serbs) were shot, beaten, or hacked to death [175; 185]. Little wonder that in these two countries the percentage of Jews killed was among the highest.

In Romania, another independent ally of Germany, the government's Jewish policy varied over time and space. Jews in the outlying provinces of Bessarabia* and Northern Bukovina* suffered especially from official and popular vindictiveness. Romania had lost these regions to the Soviet Union in June 1940; the loss had been blamed partly on the alleged treachery of local Jews, who were associated stereotypically with communism. A year later Romania joined Germany in invading the USSR and recovered the lost provinces. Much of the populace assisted the Romanian army (together with the German *Einsatzgruppe* D) in taking violent revenge, killing upwards of 160,000 Jews, while the government made plans to deport the survivors of the massacre to Transnistria*, the former Soviet territory between the Dniester and Bug Rivers now occupied by Romanian troops, as a prelude to their eventual transfer to German hands. The transfer to the Germans was never completed, but some 150,000 Jews were removed to Transnistrian camps, with 25,000 dying *en route* and another 80,000 over the next three years. On the other hand, the 250,000 Jews of the so-called Regat*, or Old Romania, were for the most part not subjected to systematic violence, except for a pogrom in Iaşi in June 1941 that claimed the lives of perhaps a third of the town's 34,000 Jewish residents. To be sure, Regat Jews suffered from increasingly severe legal restrictions, expropriation measures, and forced labour, and Jewish males from certain towns were incarcerated in detention camps. Some historians have argued that these steps were undertaken in anticipation of eventual Romanian cooperation in the Nazi killing programme. However, from late 1942 dictator Ion Antonescu*, with the support of much of the country's political and military leadership, resisted German deportation demands. This reversal was evidently caused by a growing sense that Germany would lose the war; Romania did not wish to be implicated any further in mass killing [133; 185]. Thus, where most Bukovinian and Bessarabian Jews perished, most Jews from Old Romania survived.

Among other things, the Romanian example indicates that the behaviour of local leadership groups in German-allied countries could fluctuate with changes in the tenor of the alliance. So too does the case of Hungary, although the weakening of Hungarian confidence in a German victory affected the fate of that country's Jews rather differently than did the same development in Romania. Hungarian regent Horthy insisted upon retaining control over the 725,000 Jews of his realm, which included not only Hungary proper but extensive additional territories taken from Czechoslovakia, Yugoslavia, and Romania in 1938–41. During 1941–44 his governments limited Jewish civic and economic freedoms severely and conscripted 50,000 Jews for labour service on the Soviet front (42,000 of whom lost their lives during the Soviet counter-offensive of January 1943). They were also prepared at one point to turn over 100,000 Jews from the additional territories to the Germans as forced labourers. But, aside from a single deportation of 18,000 such Jews in 1941, they did not contemplate participation in the murder plan. The situation changed abruptly, however, in March 1944: after Hungary, convinced that Germany was about to be defeated, sent out peace feelers to the West, German forces occupied the country, Horthy retired from active political involvement, and a new government, headed by the former Hungarian ambassador in Berlin and heavily influenced by German advisers, was established. This government ordered the immediate ghettoization and deportation of Hungary's Jews. Between 15 May and 9 July 1944, over 430,000 Jews were sent to Poland, mostly to the killing centre at Birkenau. A temporary respite was achieved in July, when Horthy, responding to entreaties from Western leaders and the Vatican, resumed his central role in politics, ordered a halt to the deportation of Jews from Budapest, and eventually removed the pro-German government. Two months later, though, the Arrow Cross*, a Hungarian fascist party, toppled Horthy. By that time Soviet advances made deportation of Jews to killing centres impossible, but the Arrow Cross militia randomly shot thousands of Budapest Jews, placed thousands more in slave labour camps, and forcibly marched 70,000 overland to build defenses for Vienna. In all, about 70 per cent of Hungarian Jewry was killed over a four-month interval [58; 59; 185].

No doubt the ability of local leaders in countries where local leaderships existed legally to protect or to harm Jews as they saw fit was enhanced by the Germans' relatively greater concern with the Jews in the countries that they controlled directly – most notably Poland, the Baltic states, and the Soviet regions. In these countries there was no Nazi-allied government or bureaucracy that could have affected the execution of the murder programme in any way; instead, the Germans recruited local sympathizers directly to serve as auxiliary policemen and guards at labour camps and killing centres and to assist in shooting operations. Indeed, Estonian, Latvian, and Lithuanian volunteers played a crucial role in locating Jews and handing them over to the *Einsatzgruppen*, while a German-sponsored Ukrainian militia launched pogroms on its own volition and later became an integral element in the liquidation of several ghettos [189]. A native Polish police force also was often called upon – together with Jewish ghetto policemen enlisted by the Germans – to patrol ghetto walls, round up Jews for deportation, and hunt Jews in hiding [184]. The participation of Poles in such actions, however, was roundly condemned by a highly ramified Polish civilian and military underground, which presided over what came to be called a 'secret state' [125]. This clandestine leadership – whose size, range of activities, and popular support far exceeded that of underground formations in the other occupied countries under direct German control – was in a position to do much that could affect the fate of many individual Jews, even if it could not stop the German murder campaign to the extent possible in countries with legal local leaderships: it could locate hiding places for Jews seeking to avoid deportation; provide them with food, money, and false identity papers; help them across borders to countries where the danger was less immediate; and supply arms to Jewish resistance groups. It could also take direct action to sabotage deportation transports or killing centres, and it could transmit information about mass killing abroad in a way that might arouse bystanders outside the Nazi orbit to action.

The Polish underground and the London-based Polish government-in-exile that supervised it did many of these things, although usually to only a limited extent. In late 1942 a special Council for Aid to Jews, known by the cryptonym Żegota*, was formed under Polish underground auspices to help Jews hide from their would-be executioners [*Doc. 26*]. This was the only such organization established anywhere in Nazi-occupied Europe. On the other hand, it was founded only after half of Polish Jewry had already been killed, it was chronically underfunded, and it managed in the end to assist at most only 4,000 people [106]. The Polish government-in-exile was a primary link in informing British, American, and other Western leaders about the Nazi murder programme; in fact, it was the first governmental body to confirm the programme's existence. However, it did not always transmit all the information in its possession, and it often subsumed the Jewish situation within the broader plight of the Polish people [79; 80]. The Polish military underground supplied some light arms to the Jewish Fighting Organization in Warsaw, but the supply represented only a small part of its available arsenal [104]. Accounting for these actions and their limited nature is a matter of considerable scholarly debate, with some historians stressing objective constraints on the extent to which Poles could come to Jews' aid, and others stressing subjective disinclination on the part of the Polish leadership to assist a people that it continued to regard as fundamentally alien [46; 79; 106]. In the end, in the words of one scholar, it appears that the behaviour of the Polish leadership towards Jews 'was forged out of an entire range of factors, both of principle and of self-interest, both hereditary ... and conjunctural' [80 *p. 213*].

A similar range of factors must be adduced to explain the variations in the behaviour of local non-Jewish leaders in all of the countries within the Nazi orbit. It is tempting to hypothesize a direct correlation between cooperation in the deportation of Jews and the pervasiveness of anti-Jewish prejudices among various populations, as sociologist Helen Fein did in 1979 [85]. Yet Romania and Hungary were countries where local authorities resisted deportation despite widespread popular dislike and suspicion of Jews. Moreover, these leaders' actions had much in common with those of the governments of France and Bulgaria, even though on the whole French and Bulgarian Jews enjoyed a significantly greater degree of social and political acceptance than did their Romanian or Hungarian co-religionists. In all four countries the authorities appear to have regarded retaining control over the fate of their Jews as symbolic of their own independence from Germany. But why did Slovak leaders not feel the same way? Why, too, did the Romanian dictator, like the leader of Croatia, countenance mass killing of Jews by forces under his control, while his Hungarian counterpart – a man of similar background and political beliefs – recoiled at the thought? And why did the government of Norway – a country with a minuscule Jewish population and virtually no anti-Jewish tradition – cooperate in deporting Jews almost as enthusiastically as did the authorities in Slovakia? Answers to these questions must no doubt take into account, among other things, the specific internal political and social conditions that prevailed in each country during the war years. Evaluating those conditions and relating them to the attitudes and actions of leadership groups towards Jews remains a largely unfulfilled task in contemporary Holocaust research.

But local leadership groups, whether legal or illegal, were not the only bystanders in a position to influence the fate of Jews. Individual victims and survivors, especially in the countries under direct German control, often were affected by the actions of non-Jewish neighbours acting on their own initiative. Virtually all Jews who survived in hiding or under cover of a false identity succeeded thanks to non-Jews who assisted them. Others survived because of the readiness of individuals with influence to protect them (like the German entrepreneur Oskar Schindler, who fought to prevent the deportation of his factory's Jewish workers). There were such 'righteous gentiles' in every country: over 8,000 have been recognized by Yad Vashem*, the Israeli Holocaust memorial authority – most for hiding Jews in their homes for extended periods, usually risking their lives (and their families') to do so. One study of these individuals has suggested that they came from all social classes and walks of life but shared a strong ability to withstand social pressure and a sense that helping someone in need was the only course of action they could imagine taking [181]. On the other hand, virtually every Jew in hiding lived under the constant threat of betrayal or blackmail. The case of Anne Frank and her family in Holland is probably the best-known instance of the threat becoming real, but its extent was considerable in other countries as well. The Polish Council for Aid to Jews regularly called attention to the phenomenon, noting its continual increase despite efforts to suppress it and charging that it made the Council's work impossible [*Doc. 27*].

Assistance and betrayal were both atypical phenomena, however. Although the issue has not been systematically studied for any country, it seems likely that for the large majority of individuals within the Nazi orbit the fate of their Jewish neighbours was at most a matter of peripheral concern. Thus few were likely to go out of their way either to help or to harm Jews. Such disregard, however, ultimately played into German hands: if survivors owed their lives to the willingness of non-Jews to aid them, how many victims owed their deaths to the unwillingness of other non-Jews to do the same?

BEYOND THE NAZI REALM

Another type of agent might have taken significant rescue action – the governments of Allied and neutral countries beyond the Nazi realm. Those governments had periodically protested against the persecution of German Jews before the beginning of mass killing, although on the whole they had shown only the most grudging willingness to provide sanctuary for those fleeing the Nazi terror and had taken little notice of the plight of Jews in other countries within the Nazi orbit. From late 1941 and throughout 1942 reports of mass killings reached the Soviets, the West, and outlying areas through a variety of channels. Recipients of those reports, however, faced even greater problems of imagination and analysis than did people who experienced the Nazi regime up close: officials in wartime London or Washington, working in the familiar, relatively tranquil surroundings of St James's Park or the Capitol Mall, could hardly grasp, as historian Bernard Wasserstein put it, that 'the agony of European Jewry was enacted in ... a grim twilight world where their conventional moral code did not apply' [187 *p. 357*]. Thus the Bund report of May 1942 does not appear to have had much lasting effect upon the consciousness of Allied or neutral policy-makers. Only in December 1942, following Polish underground courier Jan Karski's arrival in London, did the three principal Allies and the exile governments of nine occupied countries officially note and condemn the Germans' 'bestial policy of cold-blooded extermination' [80; 99; 132].

Karski brought to London and Washington a demand from Jewish resistance organizations in Poland to 'adjust [the strategy of war] to include the rescue of a fraction of the ... Jewish people' [16 *p. 328*]. On behalf of the Jewish leaders he asked the Allies to negotiate exchanges of Jews for German prisoners or for ransom, to drop leaflets from the air upon German cities informing the German people what their government was doing to Europe's Jews, and to send supplies (especially blank passports) that might help Jews escape or survive in hiding [81; 192]. Other Jewish spokesmen outside occupied Europe called upon Allies and neutrals to open their gates to Jewish escapees requiring temporary asylum, to warn Germans that the deportation and murder of Jews would be punished after the war, to create special government bodies to explore ongoing rescue opportunities, and to bomb the killing centre at Auschwitz-Birkenau and the rail lines leading to it.

For the most part, these demands were either ignored or rebuffed. Following their December 1942 statement, the Allies took no further official joint public notice of the German killing programme. An Anglo-American conference on refugees was held at Bermuda* in April 1943, but no action stemmed from it. A February 1943 Romanian proposal to release 70,000 Jews from Transnistria in return for payment was rejected by the British and US governments, as was an April 1944 German offer to exchange a million Jews, including all the Jews of Hungary, for 10,000 trucks and amounts of various foodstuffs. No Allied or neutral country expressed readiness to take in large numbers of Jewish exchangees or escapees (except Sweden with regard to Jews from other Scandinavian countries); in particular, British restrictions on Jewish immigration to Palestine were not lifted, and Jews attempting to make their way to the country were intercepted and imprisoned. Auschwitz was not bombed. To be sure, the US War Refugee Board*, established in January 1944, catalysed the return of the survivors of the Transnistrian camps to Old Romania the following March and helped generate the international pressure that prompted Horthy's cessation of the Hungarian deportations in July. The Board was also active in searching for havens for the minority of Europe's Jews that remained alive in the last year of the war, and it underwrote the mission of Swedish diplomat Raoul Wallenberg* to Budapest, through which some 20,000 Jews were rescued from deportation with the aid of special protective passports issued by the Swedish and other governments. However, even its chairman characterized the Board's activity as too little, too late [193].

Historians have advanced various explanations for the relative paucity of significant Allied and neutral rescue action. Some have stressed faulty perception, reiterating that the enormity and unprecedented nature of the Nazi crime prevented real understanding of the threat facing Jews (even after reliable reports of mass killing had been confirmed) and suggesting that had the shock of the news not been so great, Allied and neutral policy-makers would have accorded rescue high priority. Others, in contrast, have argued that Jewish matters would in any case not have been a central concern, whether because of the single-minded attention the combatants needed to devote to winning the war, the lack of Jewish political leverage in a situation where free-world Jewish groups would have to support the Allied cause enthusiastically in any case, or personal ill-will towards Jews on the part of certain officials in key positions [82; 173]. In fact, claimed historian Walter Laqueur, it was precisely the low priority that Allied bureaucrats gave the Jewish situation that allowed them to pass lightly over reports of mass murder without seriously considering their implications [132].

In the end, though, it appears that the Allied and neutral governments did not do more to extricate European Jews from their mortal peril because the only reason that could be adduced for them to do so was a moral one. Allies fighting a bloody and protracted war that demanded the full measure of their concentration and resources, and neutrals striving to avoid their own possible occupation, found accession to such a moral argument an unaffordable luxury. No country could see any compelling political, strategic, or legal reason to 'adjust [the strategy of war] to include' the rescue of Jews who were not its citizens. What Helen Fein called 'the organizational incapacity and unreadiness among nation-states to protect members of other nation-states' made rescue from beyond the Nazi realm a most improbable expectation [85 *p. 166*].

8 HUMANITY, MODERNITY, AND THE HOLOCAUST

The Allies claimed that they could contribute best to rescuing Jews by winning the war as quickly as possible. Indeed, in the end only the Allied victory put an end to the murder campaign. The gas chambers at Birkenau functioned until November 1944, when, in anticipation of imminent conquest by Soviet forces, the last remaining Jewish and non-Jewish prisoners from Auschwitz and other concentration and labour camps in Poland were evacuated and forcibly marched to Germany proper. Some 250,000 Jews and non-Jews died in these so-called death marches*. Those who survived spent the final weeks of the war in Dachau, Buchenwald, and other German camps, where they were liberated by British and US forces in April–May 1945. Photographs of these prisoners have become standard images of the Holocaust. At the time they were first published they were greeted with shock and disbelief. They have continued to arouse horror and fascination ever since.

This book began by suggesting that a dispassionate look at the basic facts of the encounter between the Third Reich and the Jews and their placement in a historical context might dispel the sense of mystery and bewilderment that encountering the Holocaust often sparks and render comprehensible events that could not be imagined at the time they occurred. Now, after having laid out the basic features of such a historical approach, it seems appropriate to ask to what extent that proposition has been proved.

Saul Friedländer, who has spent most of his adult life applying the tools of the professional historian in an effort to understand the Holocaust, has written of 'the unease in historical interpretation' of such a seemingly unimaginable set of events. In his words, 'for some historians ... an opaqueness remains at the very core of the historical understanding and interpretation of what happened' [91 *p. 103*]. Although the accumulation of factual knowledge in the more than five decades since the end of the Second World War is impressive, he has argued, 'there is no clearer perspective today, no deeper comprehension than immediately after the war' [93 *p. 1*].

But if so much factual knowledge has been amassed over the past half century, what exactly remains opaque? Murder investigations generally concentrate upon three questions – motive, means, and opportunity. The story of how the Third Reich, together with some of its allies, acquired the opportunity to cause the deaths of some 5.8 million Jews seems fairly straightforward: the sources of the Nazi party's accession to power in Germany, its diplomatic and military triumphs that brought almost 9 million Jews within its reach during 1933–45, and the frequent (if not unlimited) ability of German agencies to do with those Jews as they wished may still be the subject of debates over details, but in no interpretation do they appear so mysterious as to defy understanding. The same is true regarding the means of murder: no great flights of imagination are necessary to comprehend how a decision to commence mass killing, once taken, could be executed. The unease in interpretation thus would seem to be concentrated about the issue of motive. Indeed, the question of why a decision to commence systematic mass killing of Jews was taken in the first place (together with the corollary questions of when the decision was taken and by whom) has demanded by far the most strenuous efforts at solution.

Not that historical research has not made headway. On the contrary, it has revealed quite clearly the precarious logic by which, at the beginning of the twentieth century, a person prepared to question the data of his senses could infer from certain widely accepted contemporary principles of biology and anthropology that Jews were literally non-human parasites threatening all humanity and needing to be killed for the sake of human survival. It has explicated the social, psychological, and organizational dynamics and the particular historical circumstances that could turn 'ordinary men' into mass killers when prodded by a critical mass of true believers who accepted such a picture of Jews. And it has raised plausible suggestions about how, in the aftermath of the First World War, such a critical mass was generated precisely within *German* society. New facts and insights continue to be adduced constantly and to refine analysis of these matters. Historians disagree strongly, to be sure, about the relative importance of each of these factors in precipitating the decision to kill, but that such factors could, in whatever combination, have generated a Holocaust does not seem unfathomable.

Nonetheless, certain features of the Holocaust continue to remain a mystery for many historians. Though there are some dissenting voices, most scholars today believe that Nazi leaders viewed the systematic murder of Jews not as a means to any rationally understandable goal but as an *end in itself*, whose success was its own justification. They consider that such murder was intended to be *total*, to lead to the death of every single Jewish man, woman, and child within the Third Reich's reach; no Jew was ultimately to be allowed to escape. They note, too, that the decision to murder had *nothing to do with Jewish behaviour*, even in the word's broadest possible sense. The murderers were unconcerned with where particular Jews lived, what languages they spoke, how they dressed, what they believed about God, or even whether they regarded themselves as Jews or not; anyone whom German law (or the laws of Germany's allies) identified as a Jew was automatically sentenced to death by virtue of that fact alone. Finally, most historians recognize that the ultimate justification for total murder lay in the conviction that Jews were not human beings, that their very existence endangered not only Germany but humanity as a whole, and that therefore the killing of each and every one of them was imperative. The intentionalist–functionalist debate was primarily about whether this conviction had *necessarily* to lead to total murder, not about whether total murder could have been pursued in its absence; on the latter point most functionalists agreed that killing operations could not have reached the dimensions that they did without such ideological grounds.

What continues to baffle many historians about these realizations is their implication that the Third Reich operated within a *totally foreign universe of discourse*, according to rules for perceiving and conceiving reality entirely beyond the experience of any contemporary society. Saul Friedländer called attention to a speech by Himmler to senior SS officers in Poznań in October 1943 to illustrate this absolute foreignness [*Doc. 28*]. He reasoned that Himmler must have grasped that no one but Nazi initiates would ever understand how the slaughter of each and every Jew within the Reich's reach could be considered a 'page of glory' in German history; otherwise he would not have acknowledged that the glorious page could never be written. Present-day readers of the speech must thus, according to Friedländer, ultimately face it with incredulity. Although, in his words, 'on the basis of the assumption of sharing a common humanity and even a common historical experience, and thus basically common perceptions of human existence in society, we try to overcome the feeling of strangeness and horror and try to find the point of psychological identity', all such efforts are doomed to failure, for there is nothing in the experience of non-Nazis that can enable them to penetrate the

Nazi conceptual domain [91 *p. 108*]. That conceptual domain, Friedländer believes, will always remain opaque.

But does that conclusion negate the historical approach altogether? Evidently those historians who share Friedländer's position are prepared to wrestle continuously with the 'noncongruence between intellectual probing and the blocking of intuitive comprehension' [91 *p. 111*]; they continue to find value in historical research, if not as a means to ultimate understanding then at least as a tool for describing the course of the Holocaust accurately. Yet not all share it. For intellectual historian Amos Funkenstein, 'the crime committed by the Nazis was of immense proportions; the horror and the suffering transgress our capacity of imagination, but it is possible to understand them rationally. Even if the perpetrators of the crime were madmen who lost all touch with reality, a reconstruction of their mentality and patterns of action would be possible.' In the end, according to Funkenstein, the Holocaust was perpetrated by flesh and blood human beings subject to the same biological and social constraints as all other humans; indeed, 'it pointed at a possibility ... of human existence, a possibility as human as the best instances of creativity and compassion'. Thus 'historians, psychologists, sociologists, and philosophers ought to ... be guided by the reasonable expectation that they can comprehend it' [98 *pp. 302–3*].

Acknowledging the particular possibility of human existence represented by the Holocaust and facing its implications, however, can be frightening. Perhaps speaking of the Holocaust as mysterious, opaque, or inconceivable is at bottom a way of coping with the fright. Yehiel De-Nur, a Holocaust survivor and prominent fiction writer whose metaphor of Auschwitz as 'another planet' evoked the idea of opaqueness more concisely and memorably than any historian's lament about inability to comprehend, appears himself to have reached this conclusion following an especially upsetting course of introspection. In 1976, at a psychiatric clinic in Leiden, the Netherlands, he underwent therapy to uncover 'the secret of the nightmares that had visited me night after night these last thirty years'. The treatment involved injections of the hallucinogenic drug LSD, which induced a series of terrifying visions. In one he saw himself as a corpse on a truck headed to a crematorium; the truck was guarded by a 'yawning German'. 'All I know about this German', De-Nur explained, 'is that on a cold morning like this he'd certainly prefer snuggling under the covers of his warm bed without having to get up this early because of some load that has to leave for the crematorium.' This glimpse of the executioner feeling a human sensation, even one so emotionally detached from the situation, generated 'all at once an additional horror ...: if this is so, then he could have been standing here in my place, a naked skeleton in this truck, while I, I could have been standing there instead of him, on just such a cold morning doing my job delivering him and millions like him to the crematorium – and like him I, too, would yawn, because like him I'd certainly prefer snuggling under the covers of my warm bed on a cold morning like this' [121 *pp. x, 10*].

As a result of his visions – which also included one in which the smoke rising from the chimney of the Birkenau crematorium turned first into the face of Satan, then into his own face, while Satan's servants proclaimed the young victim sovereign of the universe and named him Nucleus – De-Nur repudiated the 'other planet' image, concluding that 'wherever there is humankind, there is Auschwitz; it wasn't Satan who created ... Nucleus, but you and I' [121 *p. 107*]. It was this realization that freed him from what had until then been his inability to speak of the Holocaust except through the medium of third-person fiction. The Holocaust, he seemed to suggest, is indeed imaginable and expressible, but only to those prepared radically to adjust their thinking about the fundamental nature of human beings.

Unfortunately, he did not indicate what specific adjustment is required. Indeed, beyond some rather commonplace statements about how the Holocaust demonstrates that the capacity of human beings to do evil to one another is far greater than anyone had imagined earlier, the fundamental rethinking that the Holocaust demands does not seem to have proceeded very far. Actually, the most serious attempts at rethinking have focused not upon humanity in general but upon modern humanity. Zygmunt Bauman has argued implicitly that not any human society but only one valuing 'the social norms and institutions of modernity' – rationality and science, planning and efficiency, objectivity and uniformity – is capable of conceiving and perpetrating systematic mass murder of the Nazi variety [55 *p. 87*]. What impressed him most about the Holocaust (as it had Hilberg and many others) was the role of the German bureaucracy in laying the ground-work for killing – defining Jews, keeping files on them, segregating and isolating them, and finally arranging the logistics of despatching them to the killing centres. Had there not been a bureaucracy willing and able to take on these tasks, Bauman claimed, the Holocaust could not have happened. But in his opinion, the availability of such a bureaucracy could be taken for granted, for all modern states depend for their very existence upon a large bureaucratic administration, organized and trained to control populations impersonally and impartially, according to whatever rules their state sets for them, without reflecting on the ethical implications of the rules or their administration. Thus, he suggested, any state with a modern 'bureaucracy is intrinsically *capable* of genocidal action', provided it is governed by an 'ideologically obsessed power elite' determined to enforce 'a grand vision of a better, and radically different, society' by any means necessary [*55 pp. 91, 94, 106*]. Such, for Bauman, was the Nazi leadership, but under certain conditions any leadership passionately committed to a utopian vision of a perfect society can, with bureaucratic assistance, destroy all who do not fit its scheme. Hence the Holocaust must precipitate thoroughgoing criticism of modern Western civilization.

Bauman's analysis has many supporters; it has many detractors as well. Some argue that although the Nazis may have employed modern means to perpetrate murder on such a mass scale, their motives were not modern at all: Jews were killed precisely because, having benefited most conspicuously from capitalism, rationalism, and political centralization and the concomitant ideas of individual freedom and equality, they symbolized some of the most notable features of modernity – features the Nazis vigorously denounced. This argument implies that commitment to those modern values, not criticism of them, stands as a safeguard against possible repetition of a Nazi-style total murder programme. Others deny that Jews were killed because they interfered with any particular utopian vision: what prompted the Third Reich to pursue them so relentlessly and systematically was ultimately Hitler's world-view, which represented them as a mortal danger to human survival in any form, utopian or not. Still others contend that even modern means, including bureaucracy, were not intrinsic to the Holocaust. They point out that the *Einsatzgruppen* murders in the Soviet Union and killings by shooting squads elsewhere were accomplished without benefit of any bureaucratic preliminaries of identification, segregation, and removal, and that the abandonment of the shooting method was prompted by considerations of convenience, not necessity; thus, they claim, the Germans, had they wished, could have pursued their murder programme without bureaucratic assistance at all.

Who is right? The test of any of the propositions advanced for or against the modernity thesis lies in the documentary record that historians of the Holocaust have been seeking, uncovering, and analysing for over fifty years. So too will the test of any other thesis about the implications of the Holocaust for human self-understanding that might be advanced in the future. The broad contours of that record have been outlined in the preceding pages, as have some of the difficulties the record presents. The work of discovery and analysis is still far from complete, as is the confrontation with its fundamental import. Whether these efforts will ever reach the point where the feeling of mystery and the sense of 'opaqueness at the core' will be banished altogether is doubtful. But the historical approach to the Holocaust has brought to light a significant body of knowledge that can, when perceptively and judiciously interpreted, help make the core clearer, at least for some.

PART FOUR: DOCUMENTS

DOCUMENT 1 **THE DEFINITION OF 'GENOCIDE', BY THE WORD'S INVENTOR**

By 'genocide' we mean the destruction of a nation or of an ethnic group. This new word ... is made from the ancient Greek word *genos* (race, tribe) and the Latin *cide* (killing), thus corresponding ... to such words as tyrannicide, homocide [*sic*], infanticide, etc. Generally speaking, genocide does not necessarily mean the immediate destruction of a nation, except when accomplished by mass killings of all members of a nation. It is intended rather to signify a coordinated plan of different actions aiming at the destruction of essential foundations of the life of national groups, with the aim of annihilating the groups themselves. The objectives of such a plan would be disintegration of the political and social institutions, of culture, language, national feelings, religion, and the economic existence of national groups, and the destruction of the personal security, liberty, health, dignity, and even the lives of the individuals belonging to such groups. Genocide is directed against the national group as an entity, and the actions involved are directed against individuals, not in their individual capacity, but as members of the national group. ...

Genocide has two phases: one, destruction of the national pattern of the oppressed group; the other, the imposition of the national pattern of the oppressor. This imposition, in turn, may be made upon the oppressed population which is allowed to remain, or upon the territory alone, after removal of the population and the colonization of the area by the oppressor's own nationals. Denationalization was the word used in the past to describe the destruction of a national pattern. The author believes, however, that this word is inadequate because: (1) it does not connote the destruction of the biological structure; (2) in connoting the destruction of one national pattern, it does not connote the imposition of the national pattern of the oppressor; and (3) denationalization is used by some authors to mean only deprivation of citizenship. ...

Genocide is effected through a synchronized attack on different aspects of life of the captive peoples: in the political field (by destroying institutions of self-government and imposing a German pattern of administration, and through colonization by Germans); in the social field (by disrupting the social cohesion of the nation involved and killing or removing elements such as the intelligentsia, which provide spiritual leadership ...); in the cultural field (by prohibiting or destroying cultural institutions and cultural activities; by substituting vocational education for education in the liberal arts, in order to prevent humanistic thinking, which the occupant considers dangerous because it promotes national thinking); in the economic field (by shifting the wealth to Germans and by prohibiting the exercise of trades and occupations by people who do not promote Germanism 'without reservations'); in the biological field (by a policy of depopulation and by promoting procreation by Germans in the occupied countries); in the field of physical existence (by introducing a starvation rationing system for non-Germans and by mass killings, mainly of Jews, Poles, Slovenes, and Russians); in the religious field (by interfering with the activities of the Church, which in many countries provides not only spiritual but also national leadership); in the field of morality (by attempts to create an atmosphere of moral debasement through promoting pornographic publications and motion pictures, and the excessive consumption of alcohol).

Raphael Lemkin, [19], pp. 79–80, xi–xii.

DOCUMENT 2   FROM AN EARLY SPEECH BY HITLER
             ABOUT THE JEWS

The Jew, in his role as parasite, is turning and must turn against national purity as a source of a people's strength. The Jew, who is himself more nationally pure than any other people, who has not blended in with any other race for thousands of years but has simply exploited racial interbreeding at propitious moments in order to cause other races to degenerate – this same Jew preaches day by day ... that all peoples on this earth are equal, that these peoples should be bound together in international solidarity, that no people should lay claim to any special disposition, and above all that no people has any basis to be proud of anything national. ...

First, [the Jew declares,] a race must be denationalized. First it must forget that its strength lies in its blood ..., for what the Jew needs in order to organize, build up, and maintain his definitive mastery over the world is the lowering of the racial level of the remaining peoples, so that he, as racially pure, will be the only one qualified to rule all others. This is the racial deterioration whose effects upon a host of peoples we observe even today. ...

An additional problem is that of the physical incapacitation of all races. This means that the Jew struggles to do away with everything that he finds capable of generating strength or of hardening the muscles. Above all he strives to do away with everything that he finds might make a people healthy enough to decide that it will no longer tolerate the presence of national racial criminals (that is, noxious weeds) in the midst of the racial community but will punish them with death, circumstances permitting. This is the Jew's greatest fear and worry, for even the strongest bolts upon the most secure prison are not so strong, and the prison not so secure, that a few million people cannot open them in the end. There is only one bolt that cannot be opened, and that is death; this he dreads the most, and therefore he yearns for the day when this barbaric punishment will be abolished wherever he continues to live as a race of parasites, although he employs it without mercy wherever he is already in control. (Spirited applause.)

Speech at a public meeting of the National Socialist German Workers Party in Munich, 13 August 1920, [23], pp. 411–12.

DOCUMENT 3   AN EX-NAZI EVALUATES THE ANTI-JEWISH ASPECT OF NATIONAL SOCIALISM, 1939

[T]he fight against Judaism ... is now an element in the revolutionary unsettling of the nation, a means of destruction of past categories of thinking and valuation, of destroying the liberalist economic system based on private initiative and enterprise; it is also a sop to the destructive revolutionism of the masses, a first lesson in cynicism. ... It is of functional importance only, a means and nothing more. It is the main element in propaganda. The question to be asked of it is not its meaning but its purpose. It serves mainly for the propagation, in a form assimilable by the masses, of revolutionary aims which can be harbored at first hand only by a small élite. The function of the philosophy is to keep alive the fighting character of the movement. ... Nothing is of more importance to National Socialism than the possession of 'enemies,' objects on which this pugnacity can sharpen its claws. This is the root explanation of such senseless and horrible myths as that of the totally evil character of the Jews. If there is no other enemy available there is always the Jew, whose despised figure can always be made to serve as fuel for the fighting spirit, and at the same time to keep alive the happy feeling of belonging to the company of the elect. ...

All these elements, so primitive and threadbare in their psychology, are nevertheless thoroughly effective in practice. It would be a great mistake to suppose that so cunning an individual as the German Minister of Propaganda [Goebbels] is not perfectly well aware that the atrocity propaganda against the Jews ... is preposterous nonsense, that he does not see through the racial swindle just as clearly as those compatriots of his whom it has driven out of their country. It would be simply foolish to imagine that any member of the élite truly and sincerely believes in the bases of the 'philosophy.' They have been deliberately concocted for their demagogic effectiveness and for the furtherance of the party's political aims. They have also been chosen with a cunning realization of the needs of the ... German masses. Other representations of good and evil, of hero and weakling, may 'work' in other countries; the selection for Germany was already indicated by the experience of the pan-Germans and the anti-Semitic 'racial' parties.

Hermann Rauschning, [25], pp. 22, 52–3.

DOCUMENT 4   HITLER AND HORTHY DISCUSS THE FATE
OF HUNGARIAN JEWRY, APRIL 1943

The Führer [Hitler] ... described to Horthy the German measures for rationing, which had been implemented in a completely orderly fashion. There is no black market in Germany. ... In this connection Horthy observed ... that he was not yet able to control the black market. The Führer responded that the Jews were responsible for this. ... When Horthy asked in response what he ought to do with the Jews, since he had already done so much to take away all possibilities for economic survival – after all, he couldn't kill them – the Reich foreign minister [Ribbentrop] explained that the Jews must either be destroyed or placed in concentration camps. There was no other way [to deal with them]. ... [The Führer stated that] the Jews had never had any organizational value. All of the fears that had been repeatedly expressed to him in Germany notwithstanding, everything was proceeding quite well without the Jews. Wherever the Jews were left to themselves – in Poland, for example – the most awful misery and depravity prevailed. They are simply pure parasites. In Poland these conditions have been fundamentally cleared away. Jews who did not want to work there were shot. If they couldn't work, they had to die. They were to be treated like tuberculosis bacteria who might infect a healthy body. This is not cruel if you keep in mind that even innocent creatures of nature, like rabbits and deer, have to be killed so they will do no damage. Why should we treat the animals who thought to bring us Bolshevism any better?

Record of the conversation between Hitler and the regent of Hungary, Miklos Horthy, in Klessheim Castle, 17 April 1943, [30], vol. 35, pp. 427–8.

DOCUMENT 5   A GERMAN JEWISH EDITOR ASSESSES THE
IMPACT OF THE NUREMBERG LAWS

The new laws promulgated at the Nuremberg party conference set the entire life of the Jews living in Germany not only before new tasks but also on a new plane altogether. If [in promulgating these laws] the German government was acting according to the intention of the Führer and Chancellor ' ... to create a plane ... upon which the German people could find a tolerable relationship with the Jewish people', these laws govern mainly the areas in which the German people does *not* wish to maintain relations. The fundamental positive constitutional idea [embodied in the laws] is to be found not in the legislation itself but in a commentary [on them] by the editor of the German News Agency. [It is] defined by the concept 'minority'. ...

[T]he national majority, which holds state power, cannot permanently remain unconcerned with whether the minority is respected or defamed from without or whether it is unified or splintered from within. In an authoritarian state the minority is also not able to allow the will of the individual free play. Thus the *Reichsvertretung* ... has properly placed the demand for state recognition of an autonomous Jewish leadership ... at the top of a grand programme for Jewish self-determination, along with the hope for the possibility of [continued] moral and economic existence.

Der Morgen 11: 8 (November 1935): 329–30.

DOCUMENT 6   A GERMAN JEWISH WOMAN DESCRIBES
HER EXPERIENCE IN THE EARLY NAZI
YEARS

Our gentile friends and neighbors, even people whom we had scarcely known before, came to assure us of their friendship and to tell us that these horrors could not last very long. But after some months of a regime of terror, fidelity and friendship had lost their meaning and fear and treachery had replaced them. For the sake of our gentile friends, we turned our heads so as not to greet them in the streets, for we did not want to bring upon them the danger of imprisonment for being considered a friend of Jews.

With each day of the Nazi regime, the abyss between us and our fellow citizens grew larger. Friends whom we had loved for years did not know us anymore. ... [W]e were hunted like deer. Through the prominent position of my husband [a rabbi] we were in constant danger. Often we were warned to stay away from home. We were no longer safe, wherever we went.

How much our life changed in those days! Often it seemed to me I could not bear it any longer, but thinking of my children, I knew we had to be strong to make it easier for them. From then on I hated to go out, since on every corner I saw signs that the Jews were the misfortune of the people. ... Never did anything unpleasant happen to me on the street, but I was expecting it at every moment, and it was always bothering me. ...

Almost every lesson began to be a torture for Jewish children. There was not one subject anymore which was not used to bring up the Jewish question. And in the presence of Jewish children the teachers denounced all the Jews, without exception, as scoundrels and as the most destructive force in every country where they were living. ...

The only hope we had was that this terror would not last very long. The day could not be far off when this nightmare would cease to hound the German people. How could anybody be happy in a land where 'freedom' was an extinct word, where nobody knew that the next day he would not be taken to jail, possibly tortured to death. ...

[In 1935 a Jewish doctor fled the country, leaving all that he owned behind.] A few days after the doctor had left with his family, we were invited to a friend's house. Of course the main subject of the evening was the doctor's flight. The discussion became heated. 'He was wrong', most of the men were arguing. 'It indicates a lack of courage to leave the country just now when we should stay together, firm against all hatred'. 'It takes more courage to leave', the ladies protested vigorously. 'What good is it to stay and to wait for the slowly coming ruin? Is it not far better to go and to build up a new existence somewhere else in the world, before our strength is crippled by the everlasting strain on our nerves, on our souls? Is not the children's future more important than a fruitless holding out against Nazi cruelties and prejudices?' ...

On our way home I still argued with my husband. He, like all the other men, could not imagine how it was possible to leave our beloved homeland, to leave all the duties which constitute a man's life. 'Could you really leave all this behind you to enter nothingness?' ... 'I could', I said again, 'since I would go into a new life'. And I really meant it.

Marta Appel, [27], pp. 352–4, 356.

DOCUMENT 7   **A YOUNG JEW COMMITS SUICIDE IN PROTEST OVER EXCLUSION FROM THE GERMAN NATION**

[5 April 1933]
Dear Friends,

Here is my final farewell! A *German* Jew cannot bear to live knowing that the movement to which nationalist Germany looks for salvation regards him as a traitor to the Fatherland! I leave without hatred or resentment. ... But because I do not see any way for me to take what I regard as suitable action, I shall try, by ending my life voluntarily, to shake up my Christian friends. You will be able to see by this step I am taking how things look to us *German* Jews. How much more would I have preferred to give my life for my Fatherland!

Do not be sad, but try to enlighten and help the truth to victory.

Fritz Rosenfelder, Stuttgart, [33], p. 160.

DOCUMENT 8   **A GERMAN JEWISH LEADER DESCRIBES THE 'RETURN TO JUDAISM'**

People are exploring the boundaries of their existence as Germans and Jews, and many of them ... are feeling something like this:

'The era of emancipation is at an end. Our emotional security has been shattered. Perhaps [our sense of security] actually made us insensate, too self-confident and satisfied. True, hostility to Jews was never absent, but we hardly allowed it to affect us. We saw historical developments from too one-sided a perspective to believe in any really earth-shaking convulsions. It is hard to imagine ... that equality for German Jews could ever be reinstated as it was before. But if it does not return, then we shall be forever excluded from the nation that we made our own with indescribable devotion and about which we feel, painfully, the same way today. In this state of inner uprootedness ... one inner foothold remains for us – our Jewishness. As we were rising in the surrounding society, we neglected our Jewishness all too much. Who among us continued to be familiar with our holy books? Who knew Jewish history? Who continued to keep our beautiful, gracious, ancient customs? Who bore his Jewishness, even when he knew about it, as anything more than an irrevocable, tired fate? Who experienced it any more as ... a creative force?'

[T]his path to inner contemplation and collectedness, this path of return to Jewishness, [is one] that we affirm and in which we see one of the great blessings of our time.

Eva G. Reichmann, Director, Central Association of German Citizens of the Jewish Faith, 1934, [26] p. 50.

DOCUMENT 9   A ZIONIST EXPLAINS HOW HIS MOVEMENT CAN HELP GERMAN JEWS

I shall not join the theoretical argument over whether Palestine is *the* solution to the situation of German Jews. ... But we must not ignore the fact that, unlike other programmes, Palestine is not a temporary solution or an asylum for the night. What we are doing in Palestine carries the stamp of permanence, and it is being carried out in an atmosphere of self-help and self-determination, which no other country in the world can give us. Thus our accomplishments depend largely upon planning and organization. In my opinion, such planning needs to be spread over several years, let's say a programme of three or four years. ...

The central problem facing German Jewry ... is that of converting the emigrants' assets into cash. As long as we avoid this problem we are leaving many people, whose assets exceed [in value] the amount that can be removed from Germany according to present currency laws, without a chance to escape. According to a cautious estimate, during recent months 40,000 individuals and families have applied to the Palestine Office in Berlin. Even if only a portion of them end up emigrating to Palestine, the number shows clearly how acute the issue of emigration is. It is folly not to see the problem or to think that it can be solved without agreement with the German government. ... Germany will not strain its foreign currency situation in order to make things easier for the Jews. ... [But] it appears that there is a possibility of reaching an agreement involving exchanging the emigrants' property for German exports in Palestine. ... [This would be] a solution that would satisfy the interests of all participants; it would represent real progress on the road to dealing constructively with the problem of the Jews in Germany.

Chaim Arlosoroff, *Jüdische Rundschau*, 23 May 1933.

DOCUMENT 10   A POLISH REPORT DESCRIBES
                CONDITIONS FOR JEWS AFTER THE
                GERMAN CONQUEST

From the first days of September [1939] to the present moment the fate of Jews in the occupied territories has been ... suffering, degradation, persecution, and expropriation. Both the system of exceptional laws introduced by the authorities and the unchecked actions in which the army, Gestapo, administration, and German population engage with impunity contribute to this situation. Officially Jews are the objects of discriminatory laws; in fact they are [treated as] outlaws. ...
    A ghetto was established in Warsaw in October 1940, long before then in [other towns]. ... [Establishing] the Warsaw ghetto created the problem of resettling 110,000 Jews and 70–80,000 Poles. It was similar in Łódź. The population density in the ghettos exceeds that of Chinese cities: 5–8 people occupy each room. ... Usually the ghettos are [located in] already overcrowded and filthy areas, without parks, often without sewage disposal systems, but with many buildings that are old or were ruined in the war. Communication with the ghettos is forbidden in principle. ... A high death rate is prevalent (up to 50 per day in Łódź) . ... [Closing the ghettos] separates Jews from the possibility of making a living and existing materially.
    There is glaring discrimination against Jews with regard to food supply. They are treated even worse than the Poles. Their bread ration is half that of Poles, their sugar ration one third. They have no ration cards for meat at all. They are supposed to receive potatoes, salt, and coal in the same amounts as Poles. Jewish restaurants do not receive any allocations. ...
    The free professions have been destroyed. Jewish lawyers have been completely eliminated; Jewish doctors have no right to treat Christians. ... Jews may not own pharmacies. The overwhelming majority of Jewish engineers is unemployed; the same for musicians, journalists, writers. ...
    An order by Governor Frank of 26 October 1939 imposes compulsory labour service on all male Jews between ages 14–60, with boys over 12 forced to register. ... [The labourers] are treated extremely poorly: they lack food and have wretched living conditions (in barns, cellars, etc.). ...
    The Jews are the object of indescribable mental torture. Face slapping; kicking; insulting address; ridicule; stealing furniture, furs, food reserves – these are daily occurrences. ...

'Działalność Władz Okupacyjnych na Ter. RP, 1.IX.39–1.XI.40' [Activity of the Occupation Authorities on Polish Territory, 1 September 1939–1 November 1940], Hoover Institution Archives: Poland, Ministerstwo Spraw Wewnętrznych, Box 4.

DOCUMENT 11   GOERING INSTRUCTS HEYDRICH TO
PREPARE A 'TOTAL SOLUTION' OF THE
JEWISH QUESTION

Berlin: 31 July 1941

The Reich Marshal of the Greater German Reich
Plenipotentiary for the Four-Year Plan
Chairman of the Ministerial Council for the Defence of the Reich

To: the Chief of the Security Police and the SD,
SS Major General Heydrich, Berlin:

As supplement to the task which was entrusted to you in the decree dated 24 January 1939, namely to solve the Jewish question by emigration and evacuation in a way which is the most favourable in connection with the conditions prevailing at this time, I herewith commission you to carry out all preparations with regard to organizational, factual, and financial viewpoints for a total solution of the Jewish question in those territories in Europe under German influence.

If the competency of other central organizations is touched in this connection, these organizations are to participate.

I further commission you to submit to me as soon as possible a draft showing the organizational, factual, and financial measures already taken for the execution of the intended final solution of the Jewish question.

[Signed] GÖRING

[31], vol. 13, pp. 169–70.

DOCUMENT 12 INVITATION TO THE WANNSEE
CONFERENCE

Berlin SW 11 29 Nov 1941
Prinz Albrecht Str. 8
Telephone: Local 120040
Long Distance 126421
Personal

Chief of the Security Police and the Security Service (SD)
IVB 4–3076/41 Secret (1180)
...

(Confidential)

To SS Gruppenführer Hofmann
Race and Settlement Main Office
Berlin

Dear Hofmann:
On the 31 July 1941 the Reich Marshal of the Greater German Reich commissioned me to make all necessary preparations in organizational, factual, and material respect for the total solution of the Jewish question in Europe with the participation of all interested central agencies and to present to him a master plan as soon as possible. A photostatic copy of this commission is included in this letter. Considering the extraordinary importance which has to be conceded to these questions and in the interest of the achievement of the same viewpoint by the central agencies concerned with the remaining work connected with this final solution, I suggest to make these problems the subject of a combined conversation, especially since Jews are being evacuated in continuous transports from the Reich territory, including the Protectorate Bohemia and Moravia, to the East ever since 15 October 1941.

I therefore invite you to such a conference, followed by luncheon, on 9 December 1941, 1200 hours, at the office of the International Criminal Police Commission, Berlin, Am Grossen Wannsee No. 56/58. ...

Heil Hitler!
Yours,
[Signed] HEYDRICH

[31], vol. 13, pp. 192–3.

DOCUMENT 13   AN EYEWITNESS DESCRIBES A MASS SHOOTING IN THE SOVIET UNION

One Saturday evening [8 August 1941] gentiles from nearby villages came to our town and said ... that the Germans were killing Jews – we'd better flee, disperse and hide. ... We asked grandfather: What shall we do, run away? He consulted with some of his acquaintances, the rabbi, the ritual slaughterer, and other important people, and then said not to run away, to remain where we are, nothing will happen. Perhaps young people will be taken to work, but killing – it can't be. ...

Next morning, at dawn, the town was in an uproar. A Jew came running from the nearby village of Borki. ... He shouted: 'Jews, run away, the Germans are coming to kill us'. ... That very moment we saw the Germans driving into town; they snatched that Jew at once. He barely got into town and was shot on the spot. All the Jews who had heard it began to run away and tried to hide. Grandfather said: 'You children get away. ... [N]othing will happen to me'. ... That day we made our escape, those who could manage, because the Germans had seized the town. We found refuge in a small forest, where we could hear shooting. ... The next day at daybreak we heard a lot of shooting. ...

When the shooting stopped, we began to make our way back. The gentiles we met told us that we could go ahead; the Germans had left. They killed everyone they found. Nobody was left. ...

[On 22 August 1941] we saw a lot of German policemen surrounding the ghetto. ... We realized that this time it wasn't a matter of counting us. ... A lot of Germans were there. Four or five Germans for every one of our people. This was not in order to count us. ... Then we were told: 'Death is threatening you. You will be shot; whoever wants to buy his way out should bring in whatever he owns in money or jewels that he has hidden'. They tormented us right till the end of the day. ... [But] we did not have anything. ... We had handed over everything before. ...

Then the gate of the ghetto opened and a truck moved in. Those who were strong enough climbed up by themselves, but the weak ones were thrown in. They were piled into the truck like cattle. ... The rest they made run after the truck. ...

We arrived at the place. Those who had been on the truck had already got down, undressed and stood in a row. ... It was about three kilometres away from our town. There was a hill and a little below it they had dug something like a ditch. They made us walk up to the hill, in rows of four, and ... shot each one of us separately. ... They were SS men. They carried several guns with plenty of ammunition pouches. ...

Some of the younger ones tried to run away. They hardly managed a few steps, they were caught and shot. Then came our turn. ...

[My six-year-old daughter and I] stood facing the ditch. I turned my head. He asked, 'Whom do I shoot first?' I didn't answer. He tore the child away from me. I heard her last cry and he shot her. Then he got ready to kill me. ... He turned me around, loaded his pistol, so that I could see what he was doing. Then he again turned me around and shot me. I fell down. ... I felt nothing. At that moment I felt that something was weighing me down. I thought that I was dead, but that I could feel something even though I was dead. ... I felt I was suffocating, bodies had fallen on me. ... I pulled myself up with the last bit of strength. When I reached the top I looked around but I couldn't recognize the place. Corpses strewn all over, there was no end to the bodies. ... The Germans were not there. No one was there. ...

When he shot me I was wounded in the head. I still have a big scar on my head, where I was wounded by the Germans. I got to my feet to see that horrible scene. ...

When I saw they were gone I dragged myself over to the grave and wanted to jump in. I thought the grave would open up and let me fall inside alive. I envied everyone for whom it was already over, while I was still alive. ... I ... tried to dig my way in with my hands. ... The earth didn't open up. I shouted to Mother and Father, why was I left alive? What did I do to deserve this? Where shall I go? To whom can I turn? I have nobody. I saw everything; I saw everybody killed. No one answered.

Testimony of Rivka Yoselewska at the trial of Adolf Eichmann, May 1961, [29], vol. 1, 514–18.

DOCUMENT 14   A *SONDERKOMMANDO* MEMBER
                DESCRIBES THE BEŁŻEC KILLING CENTRE

On 16 August 1942 I was taken during an *Aktion* in Lwów to the Janowska camp. The next day I was loaded onto a railroad car. ... The train carried about 5,000 people, [including] women and children ..., [in] closed, sealed freight cars with grates on the windows. ... The journey lasted seven nightmarish, desperate, hopeless hours. The train arrived at Bełżec station. ...

The camp was situated in a young coniferous forest, out of which a 3 km square clearing had been cut. ... From a distance it was invisible, because the cut trees had been lashed to the growing ones to create a thicket that blocked the light, hiding the barracks and death chambers that were located there. ...

After unloading, all were ordered to disrobe, men and women together. We were told that we were going to the baths and then to work. For a while the people were glad to hear talk about work. Dozens of Jews from the *Sonderkommando* rummaged through the clothing, removed gold and money. The clothing was taken to the warehouse; valuables were sorted and brought to the camp office.

The building in which the gas chambers were located was a single-storey bungalow painted white. A corridor ran down the middle; there were three chambers to the left, three more to the right. The building was made of concrete. There were no windows. The roof, 3.5 metres high, was covered with roofing paper.

Jewish barbers shaved the women's heads in the yard outside. The women sat naked on stools and were shorn one by one. While waiting they were beaten on the head and face with whips. The people were shoved into the 'baths' *en masse*, with no order, without counting, like cattle to be slaughtered. In the corridor people understood that they were going to die. Whoever balked was prodded with a bayonet by Ukrainian guards. ...

The gassing took twenty minutes. The gas was produced by a gasoline engine worked by two Ukrainian machinists. It was located in a room at the end of the corridor. The gas ran through pipes into the chambers. ...

The corpses were dragged by leather straps to graves 200–300 paces distant. On the way from the building to the graves, ten dentists, selected from among the prisoners, opened the corpses' mouths and extracted the teeth; later they melted the gold into ingots, which went to the camp commandant's office. ...

Immediately upon arrival skilled workers were selected – carpenters, metalworkers, cobblers, tailors. I said I was a machine fitter. I was assigned to the machine that dug sand out of the grave pits. ...

There were 500 people in the *Sonderkommando* Every day the ranks were thinned by 30–40. The Germans culled the workers who were weak, called out their names at noon, made them run to the grave, and shot them. They brought the number back to 500 out of the new transports. ...

Testimony of Rudolf Reder, [4], pp. 56–8.

DOCUMENT 15   **THE POLISH UNDERGROUND REPORTS THE LIQUIDATION OF THE WARSAW GHETTO**

In the past few days the liquidation of the Warsaw ghetto has begun. ... On 22 July [1942], notices were posted on the walls of the ghetto, according to which 6,000 Jews from Warsaw were to be resettled daily in the east. This undoubtedly signifies shipment to a place of execution. The 'resettlees' have the right to take with them 15 kg of baggage and any jewelry. The resettlement does not include employees of the community or hospitals, doctors, order police, holders of work cards, and persons certified by the medical commission as fit for work (no such commission was established). After the resettlement has been carried out, those Jews remaining in the ghetto will be quartered in barracks and put to work. That same day machine guns were stationed at the ghetto gates, and in the streets 'thugs' – Lithuanians, Latvians, Ukrainians – appeared. Shooting began at passers-by. The deportation action is carried out in the following manner: A closed apartment building is picked at random, and the Jewish police pull everyone out of it, without regard to age or state of health. After the elimination of those not subject to deportation, the remaining are transported by lorry or tram to a waiting train. Several trains (of open cars enclosed with barbed wire) have already left. Blocking off of apartment buildings is going on at several points in the city. Independently of this, acts of hooliganism – so far sporadic – have begun. The thugs force their way into apartments and shoot all present. ... The victims of the first day of the 'resettlement' action were mainly old and sick people, invalids, children, infants, women, and a large percentage of foreign Jews. The young people attempted to hide. The terrified population runs into the streets or wanders from apartment to apartment. Complete depression. Many suicides. ...

'Pro memoria o sytuacji w Kraju w okresie 1–25 lipca 1942 r.' [Memorandum on the situation in Poland, 1–25 July 1942], Polish Underground Study Trust, London, 56/113.

DOCUMENT 16   AN EARLY ASSESSMENT OF GERMAN POLICY TOWARDS JEWS IN OCCUPIED POLAND

The Germans are attempting at all costs to win over the Polish masses. ... They are attempting [to persuade the masses that] 'the Germans, and the Germans alone, will help the Poles to settle accounts with the Jews'.

Thus the relation of the Germans to the Jews clearly exceeds the strictures of their official ideology and is *one of the elements of their internal policy.*

They are attempting:

1) to extract as much as they can from the Jews (money, stocks, means of production, workshops);

2) to cleanse the lands seized by them of Jews, at the price of Judaizing the Generalgouvernement;

3) to use the Jews as bait to win the sympathy, recognition, and respect of broad strata among the Poles.

'At last the Germans are solving the Jewish question in the Generalgouvernement, not so much for themselves as in consideration of the interest of the Polish nation' – this is how, according to the German design, the [Polish] populace ought to understand their behaviour.

Much indicates that it is indeed this that they desire.

They do not particularly care *in principle* about the oppression of Polish Jews in the Generalgouvernement:

A Jew can still buy himself out of wearing an armband or patch if he has a lot of money; he can still go over to the Bolsheviks if he pays; often he can even still get a passport if he gives a bribe. The Germans are not resettling Jews from Zakopane as they had announced, since the Jewish community paid them ransom; they still are not arresting important rabbis or other Jewish personalities when they pay for their freedom; etc., etc. ...

Plunder, 'the psychological outlet of the Master Race', and the duping of the Polish populace – these are their real goals.

Jan Karski, February 1940, [8], pp. 11–12.

DOCUMENT 17   THE STORY OF A MASS SHOOTING IS MET WITH DISBELIEF

The Germans occupied Wilno on 24 June 1941. They entered the ghetto on 6 September. During these two and a half months, about 40,000 Jews disappeared from Jewish Wilno. ... The Germans said they were taking the Jews to the labour camp of Ponary. But the Poles were saying that they heard shots at Ponary. Ponary is a beautiful forest beyond Wilno. ...

I was at the time a doctor in Wilno. ... One morning I saw in the street a woman with dishevelled hair, barefoot, walking with flowers in her hands and giving the impression of a woman who had gone out of her mind. The woman came into my room and said to me: 'I have come from Ponary'. I asked: 'Have you come from the labour camp at Ponary?' She said: 'No, it is not a labour camp. They are killing the Jews there'. She described how, on the night of 31 August 1941, she was brought there together with ... about ten thousand Jews. ... She heard the sound of shots. [Wounded,] she fell into the pit. ... She remained amongst the dead bodies until sunset. And that night ... she got out from amongst the bodies. She crossed the barbed wire fence, escaped, ran through the forest until she came to a little valley, and there she found a simple Polish peasant woman. The peasant woman made a bandage for her from a towel, gave her flowers in her hand and said to her: 'Run away from here, but go with the flowers as if you are a plain peasant woman, so that they should not realize that you are a Jewess'. And then she came up to me and opened the towel-bandage and I saw the wound, the bullet hole, and ants were crawling in the hole – ants of the forest.

Then I realized the truth about Ponary. I went out into a street. ... I turned to the Jews and said: 'Jews, Ponary is not a labour camp – in Ponary they are killing Jews'. And they said to me: 'Doctor, you too are creating a panic? Instead of consoling us, instead of encouraging us, instead of giving us hope, you tell us horror tales – that there are killings in Ponary? How could it be that they should simply take Jews and kill them?'

Testimony of Mark Dworzecki at the trial of Adolf Eichmann, May 1961, [29], vol. 1, 447–8.

DOCUMENT 18   THE FIRST JEWISH INTUITION OF A NAZI MURDER PROGRAMME

Abba: Since our last meeting ... our nearest and dearest have been torn from us and led to death with masses of other Jews. ... With the uprooting of our comrades the naked truth stands before us. That truth says that we must not believe that those who have been taken from us are still alive, that they have merely been deported. Everything that has befallen us to this point means ... death. Yet even this fact is not the whole truth. ... The destruction of thousands is only a harbinger of the annihilation of millions. Their death is our total ruin.

It is still difficult for me to explain why Wilno is bleeding while Białystok is peaceful and calm. ... But one thing is clear to me: Wilno is not just Wilno. [The shootings at] Ponary are not just an episode. The yellow patch is not the invention of the local SS commander. This is a total system. We are facing a well-planned system that is hidden from us at the moment.

Is there any escape from it? No. If we are dealing with a consistent system, fleeing from one place to another is nothing but an illusion. ... Is there a chance that we might be rescued? Cruel as the answer may be, we must reply: no, there is no rescue! ... Maybe for dozens or hundreds; but for the ... millions of Jews under the yoke of German occupation there is no rescue.

Is there a way out? Yes. There is a way out: rebellion and armed resistance. ...

Adam: ... How can we, in our present state, think of ... armed resistance when we know that this might precipitate the great, final catastrophe. After all, we have no assurance that we are facing the immediate absolute liquidation of the ghetto, its total annihilation. Once we begin our action will we not be endangering the entire ghetto? ... Do we have the right to assume responsibility for all Jews, to endanger their lives and to hasten their destruction if we fail? None of the ghetto Jews will stand with us; no one will understand us. They may even curse us and turn against us, for they will think that we are the source of the disaster that is befalling them. ... Collective responsibility hangs over our head like a sword of Damocles. ...

Abba: The unresolved point in the discussion is: How can we be certain that we are facing complete physical extermination? To me the matter is clear enough, but I shall not be able to convince the others. Only the last one of us who remains alive can be completely certain. But anyone who observes what is happening around us with a clear mind, and open heart, and mainly with a healthy instinct, cannot help but be convinced: we are headed for absolute, total annihilation. The day will come when that recognition will be common to all, but what is important is that it not come too late. ... Thus we must choose to act as if we were certain, despite the doubts.

From a meeting of the Wilno leadership of the Zionist youth movement *Hashomer Hatsair*, December 1941, [18], pp. 49–51.

DOCUMENT 19   A JEWISH UNDERGROUND PARTY
INFORMS THE POLISH GOVERNMENT-IN-
EXILE OF A PLAN TO MURDER ALL POLISH
JEWS

From the day the Russo-German war broke out, the Germans embarked upon the physical extirpation of the Jewish population on Polish soil, using Ukrainians and Lithuanians for that purpose. This began in the summer months of 1941, first in eastern Galicia. ... In Lwów 30,000 Jews were murdered, in Stanisławów 15,000, in Tarnopol 5,000, in Złoczów 2,000, in Brzeżany 4,000. ...

In October–November the same thing began to happen in Wilno and environs and in the Kaunas area in Lithuania. During November 50,000 Jews were murdered in Wilno. At present there are 12,000 Jews there. According to various estimates, the overall number of Jews in the Wilno and Kaunas regions who have been bestially murdered reaches 300,000. ...

In November–December the murder of Jews in Polish territories annexed to the Reich (the so-called Warthegau) began. Murder was carried out here by means of gassing, which was done in the village of Chełmno. ... A special motor vehicle (gas chamber), into which ninety people were loaded at a time, was used for gassing. The victims were buried in special dumping pits in the Lubardzki forest. ... Between November 1941–March 1942, the Jews of Koło, Dąbie, Bugaj, and Izbica Kujawska (altogether 5,000 people), plus 35,000 Jews from the Łódź ghetto and a certain number of Gypsies, were gassed at Chełmno.

In February 1942 the extirpation of the Jews began in the so-called Generalgouvernement. It started in Tarnów and Radom, where Gestapo and SS-men began visiting the Jewish quarters daily, systematically killing Jews in streets, courtyards, and apartments. In March the massive expulsion of Jews from Lublin began, during whose course children and old people in the orphanages and old-age homes, as well as patients in the general and communicable disease hospitals, were brutally murdered. ... About 25,000 Jews were transported from Lublin in sealed railroad cars 'in an unknown direction'; all trace of them has been lost. About 3,000 Jews were housed in barracks in Majdanek Tartarowy, a Lublin suburb. In Lublin there is no longer a single Jew. ...

Since 18 April [Gestapo officers] have been killing a number of Jews [in Warsaw] daily in broad daylight, at home or outside. This action is conducted according to prepared lists and encompasses all places where Jews move about in the Warsaw ghetto. There is talk of more bloody nights. According to an estimate, to date the Germans have murdered 700,000 Polish Jews.

These facts demonstrate irrefutably that the criminal German regime has begun to realize Hitler's prediction that five minutes before the end of the war, no matter how it ends, he will murder all the Jews of Europe. ... Immediate annihilation threatens millions of Polish citizens of Jewish nationality.

Therefore we ask the Polish Republic, as the protector and representative of all people living on Polish territory, immediately to take the necessary steps to prevent the annihilation of Polish Jewry. To this end the Polish Republic must exert its influence upon the Allied governments and the responsible agents in those countries immediately to apply a policy of reprisal against German citizens. ... [The German government] must know that Germans in the United States and other countries will have to answer *now* for the bestial extirpation of the Jewish population.

We understand that we are demanding extraordinary steps from the Polish Republic. This is the only way to save millions of Jews from certain annihilation.

May 1942

'Raport Bundu w sprawie prześladowań Żydów' [Bund report on the persecutions of Jews], Hoover Institution Archives: Stanisław Mikołajczyk, Box 12.

DOCUMENT 20   THE WARSAW *JUDENRAT* OFFERS TO
                REGULATE JEWISH FORCED LABOUR

[*The following description was written by Szmul Zygielbojm, a member of the Warsaw* Judenrat, *following his escape from Poland in December 1939.*]

One of the most awful torments picking away at Jewish life in Poland under the Nazis is kidnapping for labour service. The Germans are seizing old and young in the streets and carrying them away to perform the hardest labour. ... When this happens Jews are brutally beaten with regularity and often murdered. ...

[The day after the Germans entered Warsaw] lorries parked near the places where Jews were standing in long rows to obtain a piece of bread. Nazis in blue uniforms, holding rifles, revolvers, and whips, undertook to cleanse the queues of Jews. Jewish women, young and old, were beaten out of the queues with fists, pulled out by the hair, knocked out with kicks to the stomach. Jewish men were grabbed by the collar, dragged out of the queues and thrown onto the dark, sealed lorries. ...

That was the beginning. Where the people were being taken, what would happen to them – no one knew. ...

[Since then] groups of Germans stand on street corners, looking at the faces of passersby. Whoever is a Jew is ordered, 'Jew, come here!' When that happens he is already lost, a captive. Often young Polish antisemites stand with the Germans and help the Nazis recognize who is a Jew. The honest Poles are angry about this. ...

I will never forget the faces of some Jews who came to the *Judenrat* offices to tell about the horrors. ... One ... was one of the best-known and finest Yiddish actors. His clothes were torn and smeared with mud and blood. His hands were cut and torn from the hard labour he was forced to perform. ... [Another] banged his fist against his own face and wailed ..., 'Look! I'm being forced to soak myself in blood. ... I won't survive this! Help, do something, help save me from this, because I'm liable to commit some horrible deed'. ...

We [in the *Judenrat*] could not bear the humiliating kidnapping of Jews from the streets the way dogcatchers catch dogs. We tried to figure out how to counteract this. The Warsaw *Judenrat* approached the Gestapo with a proposal: if the German occupation authorities need people for labour, they should obtain them in an organized fashion; but the kidnapping of people in the streets must stop. Let the daily quota of Jews required by the Germans be determined, and the community will provide people.

The Gestapo accepted the proposal on the surface. From that time (November 1939) the Warsaw *Judenrat* did indeed provide two thousand Jews a day for labour service. But the kidnapping of Jews from the streets did not stop.

When the community protested, the Gestapo replied ... that the military authorities were the ones doing the kidnapping, and the Gestapo had no control over them. Nonetheless, the obligation that the *Judenrat* had undertaken remained in force: it had to continue providing two thousand workers every day, even though kidnappings from the street went on anyway.

S.M. Zygielbojm, 'M'khapt oyf arbet' [Kidnapping for labour], [11], pp. 142–50.

DOCUMENT 21   THE LEADER OF THE BIAŁYSTOK *JUDENRAT* PREACHES 'SALVATION THROUGH WORK'

Today's meeting is being held under the severe impression of the events of the last weeks [the mass deportations from Warsaw and Slonim]. We must not shut our eyes to our own fate; we must face the truth squarely.

Białystok has been living a more or less peaceful life during the past year. ... Our task is to maintain that situation and to extend it to the end, which has to come someday.

But by what available means ... can we do this? ... We cannot simply come and say, 'We want to live, we have wives and children'! There is no pity. There is only one recourse: deeds! [We must] turn the ghetto into an element that is too valuable, too useful to destroy.

And we are doing this.

You yourselves have seen how in recent weeks ... delegations have come here. Some have included the highest ranks in the regime. They are coming ... to resolve the question of whether the ghetto should exist. These are the days when our fate will be determined. ... We have now put 40 percent of the Jewish population – almost all who are physically able – to work. This makes a powerful impression and to a certain extent blunts the hostile actions of our enemies. ...

Efraim Barash, 16 August 1942, [3], p. 236.

DOCUMENT 22   THE HEAD OF THE ŁÓDŹ GHETTO
ANNOUNCES THE DEPORTATION OF
CHILDREN

The ghetto has been hit with a painful blow. They are demanding from us our most precious fortune – children and the elderly. I was not privileged to have a child of my own, so I gave the best years of my life to children. ... In my old age I must stretch out my hands and beg: 'Brothers and sisters, turn them over to me! Fathers and mothers, give me your children'. ...

Yesterday I was commanded to expel twenty-odd thousand Jews from the ghetto, and if not – 'We will do it!' And the question presented itself: 'Should we take over and do it ourselves or leave it for others to carry it out?' Thinking not about how many will perish but about how many might be saved, we ... came to the conclusion that, no matter how hard it is for us, we should take it upon ourselves to execute the evil decree.

I must perform this difficult and bloody operation. I must amputate limbs in order to save the body! I must take children because, if not, others could be taken as well, heaven forbid. ...

In the ghetto we have many tuberculosis patients whose life expectancy is numbered in days, or maybe in weeks. I don't know – maybe this is a devilish plan, maybe not – but I can't hold it back: 'Give me those sick people, and in their place we can save healthy ones'. ... Each evil decree forces us to weigh and measure: who should, can and may be saved? And common sense dictates that the ones to be saved must be those ... who have a chance of being rescued, not those who cannot be saved in any case.

Remember that we live in the ghetto. Remember that our life is so constricted that we do not have enough even for the healthy, let alone for the sick. Every one of us feeds the sick at the expense of our own health: we give up our bread to the sick. ... And the result of all this is not only that the sick don't get better but that we become sick ourselves. ...

Standing before you is a broken Jew. Don't be jealous of me. This is the worst decree I have ever had to carry out. I stretch out my broken, trembling hands to you and beg: Place the victims in my hands so that they can help us avoid having further victims and protect a community of a hundred thousand. So I have been promised: if we deliver our victims by ourselves, we shall have quiet. ...

What do you want, for 80–90,000 Jews to survive or for everyone to perish, heaven forbid? ... Judge me as you will; my obligation is to protect the remaining Jews

Mordechai Haim Rumkowski, 4 September 1942, [32], pp. 311–14.

DOCUMENT 23 A WARSAW GHETTO RESIDENT COMMENTS
ON CZERNIAKÓW'S SUICIDE

The chairman of the *Judenrat*, engineer Adam Czerniaków ..., refused to sign
the [deportation] order. After a conference with the authorities on the second
day of the action, 23 July, the bold and resourceful Adam Czerniaków committed suicide. ... He was found dead in the *Judenrat* office. Clearly he had
not wanted to put his own name to the deportation (it is rumoured that the
Germans announced publicly that they had begun deporting Jews from Warsaw at the *Judenrat*'s behest!). Czerniaków had not wanted to be a witness to
this tragedy, whose extent he certainly foresaw. He did a bad thing, for following his departure almost 400,000 people were left without leadership. In
my opinion he should have foreseen this and demonstrated even greater courage by staying alive. Perhaps he no longer had the strength. ...

At the time we were stupid. The shock of Czerniaków's death made us
think not that he had been brave but that he had had a nervous breakdown,
and we dismissed any thought of extermination as unreal and impossible.

From the secret journal of Henryk Makower, [21], p. 56.

DOCUMENT 24 SELF-HELP AND ALTERNATIVE
LEADERSHIP IN WARSAW

In the building where I lived there were 30 needy families. ... They occupied a
boarded-up office at the rear of the building, where there was no electricity,
gas, or water. ... They stubbornly battled the harsh conditions of life as best
they could. [But] prices soared, and their strength and reserves became
exhausted. ... A house committee organized to get food for the children, distributed holiday gift packages, bought medicines, summoned doctors, set up a
club in a heated room where they could sit by day, tried to find clothing,
sought employment for those able to work, and gave grants or loans whenever possible. Several dozen house committees organized a people's kitchen ...
that distributed several hundred portions of soup daily to the neediest.

The house committees ... often played an important role ... in building
people's political awareness. The *Judenrat* opposed the house committees,
because it could not control the activities of so many such bodies. It wanted
to transform them into organs of administrative pressure.

From an unknown author's ghetto journal, [10], pp. 41–2.

DOCUMENT 25   HIDING IN A BUNKER

We thought about arranging a hiding place; but building a bunker was not easy, for our hut was not detached and had no basement. There was a tiny table next to the kitchen stove. The floorboard that ran between the legs of the table could be removed easily. Underneath the board we gouged out a hole and covered it so that those who didn't know about it couldn't notice anything. But we had to do everything in such a way that the floorboards would have dirt underneath them, so that they wouldn't make a hollow sound, different from the rest of the floor. We managed with great difficulty to remove many buckets of dirt. Finally the bunker was ready. There was enough room in the cave under the floor for four people to squeeze in tolerably. On one side we dug out a recess, where we put the floorboard and some water, and even a small thermos. Thus we passed many nights and days in terror.

Testimony of Wiktor Littner, [4], pp. 155–6.

DOCUMENT 26   ŻEGOTA APPEALS FOR FUNDS TO RESCUE POLISH JEWS

To the [Polish] Minister of Social Welfare, London:

The occupier's murder of the country's Jewish population, which is increasing daily and now reaching culmination, imposes ever greater and more difficult obligations ... for rescuing the remaining ... Jews and supporting active resistance units. In the fourth year of the war the Polish people have become so impoverished that, although we can demand that they give their lives to aid and hide hunted Jews ... it is impossible to demand ... material contributions. ... The Council for Aid to Jews ... possesses so relatively few material resources received from the [underground authorities] that they represent only symbolic assistance in the face of the enormity of the demands and needs that mount each day. The Council ... has already requested the Polish government-in-exile ... to send it 6–8 million zł. per month if assistance is to be real and not a fiction. Unfortunately, so far the Council has received neither assistance nor a response.

The prime minister's words ... about extending aid to the ill-fated Jewish population found a lively response here ..., but in order for documents to remain of large-scale humanitarian activity by the Polish population ... great amounts of funds are needed for establishing aid centres, for continuous and not merely haphazard assistance to the victims, for the inclusion of as many victims as possible, and for reaching wherever aid is needed, wherever it is still possible to release a person from the hands of the criminals.

Thus the Council for Aid to Jews ..., conscious of its obligations and responsibilities ..., asks you to intervene in this matter, to allocate the needed funds for this purpose, and to send the Council a response as quickly as possible.

The Council's future plans depend on this.
Warsaw, 12 May 1943

Yad Vashem Archives, O6/48.10a

DOCUMENT 27   A PLEA TO COMBAT BLACKMAIL OF JEWS
IN HIDING

The plague of blackmail carried out by criminal elements of society against
Jews ... is already a mass phenomenon. ...

A determined struggle against this hideous practice of extorting and
denouncing the victims of German terror is becoming the burning problem of
the moment, and the condemnation of this disgraceful plague is a matter of
our community's honour and self-respect.

The Aid Council Żegota, at its meeting on 25 [March 1943], decided to
request of the government delegate:

1. Publication and posting of death sentences against blackmailers that
have already been carried out. Only street placards including the grounds for
the sentences and a categorical admonition against other [such deeds] will
create the necessary effect and bring real results. Only in this way will the
broad mass of the populace realize that the government delegate regards
blackmail as a capital crime. ...

2. Stepping up the active struggle against blackmailers by ... regularly
assigning ... the death penalty. Such a decisive stand by state officials will
undoubtedly bring the expected result and radically change the demoralizing
state of affairs.

Żegota petition to the Polish underground leadership, March 1943, [24], pp.
370–1.

DOCUMENT 28   HIMMLER COMMENTS ON MASS MURDER

I ... want to speak to you ... of a really grave chapter. Amongst ourselves ... it
shall be said quite openly, but all the same we will never speak about it in
public. ...

I am referring ... to the extermination of the Jewish people. ... Most of you
men know what it is like to see 100 corpses side by side, or 500, or 1,000. To
have stood fast through this and ... to have stayed decent – that has made us
hard. This is an unwritten and never-to-be-written page of glory in our history. ... All in all ..., we can say that we have carried out this most difficult of
tasks in a spirit of love for our people. And we have suffered no harm to our
inner being, our soul, our character.

From a speech to senior SS officers, Poznań, 4 October 1943, [2], pp. 344–5.

CHRONOLOGY

1933

30 January	Adolf Hitler appointed Chancellor of Germany
9 March	Nazi party militias begin wave of anti-Jewish street violence throughout Germany
1 April	Nazi regime sponsors one-day boycott of Jewish businesses
7 April	Law for the Restoration of the Professional Civil Service enacted
16 June	German Jewish Cultural Association founded
17 August	Haavara agreement concluded
8 September	Jewish organizations meeting in Geneva call for worldwide boycott of German products
17 September	Reichsvertretung founded
17 October	Law bans Jews from working for German newspapers

1934

2 August	Upon the death of German President Hindenburg, Hitler becomes sole leader of Germany

1935

15 September	Nuremberg Laws proclaimed

1938

13 March	Germany annexes Austria
26 April	German government issues instruction confiscating Jewish businesses and requiring registration of Jewish-owned property
5–15 July	Evian Conference
26 August	Central Office for Jewish Emigration established in Vienna
27 September	Jewish barristers banned from appearing in court
28 October	14,000–17,000 Jewish residents of Germany with Polish citizenship deported to Poland
7 November	Herszel Grynszpan, a Jewish student in Paris whose

	parents were deported from Germany to Poland, shoots a German embassy official in revenge
9–10 November	German government organizes Kristallnacht, ostensibly as collective punishment of Germany's Jews for Herszel Grynszpan's action

1939

13–15 March	Germany occupies Czechoslovakia, creating the Protectorate of Bohemia and Moravia and the satellite state of Slovakia
17 May	British White Paper restricts Jewish immigration to Palestine to average of 15,000 per year for five years
22 June	Jewish Emigration Office opened in Prague
4 July	Reichsvereinigung replaces Reichsvertretung.
1 September	Germany invades Poland, conquering the country within a month
17 September	Soviet army occupies eastern Poland
21 September	Heydrich orders relocation of small Polish Jewish communities and establishment of Jewish councils
12 October	Authorities in Vienna and the Protectorate deport first transports of Jews to Nisko reservation
26 October	Jews in Generalgouvernement made subject to forced labour
28 November	First ghetto established in Piotrków Trybunalski

1940

9 April	Germany occupies Denmark and southern Norway
10 May	Germany invades Holland, Belgium, and France; Łódź ghetto sealed
10 June	Italy enters war on German side
22 June	France signs armistice with Germany and leaves war
3 October	Vichy French government enacts anti-Jewish legislation
15 November	Warsaw ghetto sealed
24 November	Hungary, Romania, and Slovakia join Axis
December	Emmanuel Ringelblum establishes secret Warsaw ghetto documentation project

1941

12 February	Germans force establishment of countrywide Jewish council (Joodse Rad) in Holland
March	Adolf Eichmann appointed head of RSHA Jewish Affairs Section
22 June	Germany invades Soviet Union
23 June	First mass killings of Soviet Jews
28 June	Pogrom in Iaşi (Romania)

31 July	Göring orders Heydrich to arrange 'final solution of the Jewish question'
15 September	First deportations to Transnistria
28–29 September	Mass shootings kill 33,771 Kiev Jews
8 December	Gas vans begin operation at Chełmno
31 December	First Jewish armed resistance unit formed in Wilno ghetto

1942

20 January	Wannsee Conference
March	First killings of Jews by gas at Sobibór, Bełżec, and Birkenau
17 March–21 April	Liquidation of Lublin ghetto
26 March	First deportation of Slovakian Jews to Auschwitz-Birkenau
28 March	First deportation of French Jews to Auschwitz-Birkenau
May	Bund tells Polish government-in-exile that Germans are engaging in 'the physical extirpation of the Jewish population on Polish soil'
17 July	First deportation of Dutch Jews to Auschwitz-Birkenau
22 July–12 September	265,000 Jews sent from Warsaw ghetto to Treblinka
28 July	Jewish Fighting Organization formed in Warsaw ghetto
5 August	First deportation of Belgian Jews to Auschwitz-Birkenau
November	German military advances halted at El-Alamein and Stalingrad; war turns in Allies' favour
10 December	First deportation of German Jews to Auschwitz-Birkenau
17 December	Allies condemn German murders of Jews

1943

15 March	First deportation of Greek Jews to killing centres
20–29 March	Bulgaria deports Jews from Thrace and Macedonia
19 April–8 May	Warsaw ghetto uprising
23 September	Liquidation of Wilno ghetto
2 October	Rescue of Danish Jewry

1944

15 May	First deportation of Hungarian Jews to Auschwitz-Birkenau
6 June	Allied invasion of Normandy
13 July	Soviet army liberates Wilno; Kaunas ghetto liquidated
23 July	Soviet army liberates Majdanek
30 August	Łódź ghetto liquidated
31 October	Deportation of Slovakian Jews to Auschwitz-Birkenau resumed

| 8 November | Death march of Budapest Jews |

1945

| 17 January | Auschwitz evacuated; prisoners begin death march |
| 8 May | Germany surrenders. |

GLOSSARY AND GUIDE TO CHARACTERS

Aktion (pl. *Aktionen*) An operation leading to the killing of Jews, most commonly involving a mass round-up and removal to a killing site.

Antonescu, Ion (1882–1946) Romanian general and dictator of the pro-German 'national legionary state', 1940–44. He ordered the mass murder of Jews in Bukovina and Bessarabia and the deportation of survivors to Transnistria, but he also prevented the killing of the Jews of Old Romania (the Regat) and southern Transylvania.

Arlosoroff, Chaim (1899–1933) Zionist leader and head of the Political Department of the Jewish Agency for Palestine. In 1933 he began negotiations with the Nazi government to permit German Jews to emigrate *en masse* to Palestine and to retain their property. These negotiations resulted in the Haavara agreement.

Arrow Cross Radical right-wing Hungarian party founded by Ferenc Szálasi in 1939. It opposed the conservative Hungarian governments appointed by Miklos Horthy and was suppressed by them, even though those governments, like the Arrow Cross, favoured alliance with Nazi Germany. When Horthy sought to abandon the German alliance, the Arrow Cross militia, supported by German troops, staged a *coup d'état*. Once in control, the Arrow Cross began shooting, incarcerating, and deporting what remained of Hungarian Jewry. It is estimated that over 80,000 Jews fell victim to Arrow Cross violence.

Asocials Nazi term referring to habitual criminals, vagrants, and beggars. Believing that criminality and vagrancy were hereditary, the Nazi regime incarcerated and sterilised many whom they branded 'asocial' without reference to any specific crime.

Auschwitz German camp complex near the town of Oświęcim, in occupied Poland, 50 km west of Kraków. The main camp (Auschwitz I) was opened in June 1940 to house Polish political prisoners. A larger satellite camp, Birkenau (Auschwitz II), was built in late 1941, and a labour camp in the nearby village of Monowice (Monowitz or Auschwitz III) was operated by the IG-Farben chemical concern from May 1942. The Auschwitz complex became the largest and most notorious of all Nazi camps. Because almost 1.5 million Jews were put to death in the killing centre at Birkenau, Auschwitz has become a primary symbol of the Holocaust.

Barash, Efraim (1892–1943?)   Head of the *Judenrat* in the Białystok ghetto.

Bełżec   German killing centre on the Lublin–Lwów rail line. Some 600,000 Jews, mostly from ghettos in Poland, were killed there between March and December 1942.

Bermuda Conference   Anglo-American conference on refugees held on the Caribbean island of Bermuda on 19–30 April 1943. It was marked mostly by disagreements between the parties and the fear that concerted action to rescue Jews from Nazi-controlled Europe would interfere with the Allied war effort. The only substantive decision taken was to extend the mandate of the Intergovernmental Committee on Refugees that had been established at the Evian Conference of 1938.

Bessarabia   Romanian–Soviet border region between the Prut and Dniester Rivers. Mostly under Russian rule during the nineteenth century, it was awarded to Romania by the Paris Peace Conference in 1919. Soviet forces annexed the area in June 1940, but Romania reclaimed it in the wake of the German invasion of the USSR a year later. In anticipation of the reconquest, Romanian dictator Antonescu secretly ordered mass killings of the province's more than 200,000 Jews, who were charged with disloyalty. Well over half were killed in combined Romanian–German operations during July–August 1941. The remaining Jews were deported to Transnistria beginning in September 1941; many thousands died *en route*.

Birkenau   Satellite camp of Auschwitz, known also as Auschwitz II, about 3 km from the main Auschwitz camp. It also functioned as the largest of the Nazi killing centres: almost 1.5 million Jews, 16,000 Soviet prisoners of war, and 20,000 Gypsies were killed there between January 1942 and November 1944. It was the primary killing centre to which non-Polish, non-Soviet Jews were deported.

Bukovina   Former duchy of the Habsburg Empire, extending from the northeast end of the Carpathian Mountains to the Dniester River, awarded to Romania by the Treaty of St Germain (1919). The USSR annexed the northern half of the province in June 1940; Romania recovered it in June 1941. Like the Jews of Bessarabia, Bukovinian Jews were charged by the Romanians with supporting the Soviet enemy and subjected to revenge attacks by the Romanian army (together with German forces). Local Ukrainians also instigated pogroms against Jews. Over 20,000 Jews were killed in this fashion; another 57,000 were deported to Transnistria.

Bund   Jewish socialist party founded in 1897. In interwar Poland it was one of the largest Jewish political movements, and it played an important role in underground activities in the Polish ghettos. Its report of May 1942 included the first statement that the Germans had a programme to kill all Polish Jews.

Central Office for Jewish Emigration   Nazi-sponsored bureau established in Vienna in August 1938 to increase the pace of Jewish emigration from Austria. A similar bureau was established in Germany in January 1939 and in the Protectorate of Bohemia and Moravia in July 1939.

Chełmno   The first Nazi killing centre. Located about 50 km west of Łódź, it employed sealed lorries for killing Jews by asphyxiation from exhaust fumes. Between December 1941 and March 1943 320,000 people were murdered there, mainly Jews from western Poland.

Concentration camps   Camps employed for incarcerating political prisoners, 'asocials', and others deemed undesirable by the Third Reich because of their beliefs, behaviour, or presumed racial inferiority. They were not killing centres of the type used for mass murder of Jews (although concentration camps were located next to the killing centres at Auschwitz and Majdanek).

Czerniaków, Adam (1880–1942)   Head of the Warsaw *Judenrat*. In July 1942 he committed suicide rather than post an order for deporting Jews from the ghetto, although he did not warn Jews of the danger that faced them.

Death marches   Forced marches of prisoners over long distances, accompanied by brutal treatment. The term is most commonly applied to the march from Budapest to Vienna in November 1944 and to the westward march of prisoners from labour and concentration camps east of Berlin during the first four months of 1945, in flight from the advancing Soviet army.

Eichmann, Adolf (1906–62)   SS official, central architect of the German murder programme. In 1938–39 he headed the Central Offices for Jewish Emigration in Vienna and Prague. Later he was appointed head of Jewish affairs for the RSHA. He supervised the logistics of deporting Jews from throughout Europe to the killing centres.

Einsatzgruppe (pl. *Einsatzgruppen*)   Special task forces under SS supervision, deployed first in Poland and later in the Soviet Union for eliminating potential resistance to German rule. During the invasion of the Soviet Union in 1941, they bore a major part of the responsibility for carrying out mass shootings of Jews.

Evian Conference   International conference on refugees, July 1938. Representatives of 32 countries came together in an effort to coordinate plans to absorb Jewish and other refugees from Germany. The conference established the Intergovernmental Committee on Refugees, but it generated virtually no practical results.

Frank, Hans (1900–46)   Head of the Generalgouvernement in Poland, 1939–45.

Generalgouvernement   German-controlled territory carved out of Poland, incorporating the districts of Kraków, Lublin, Radom, and Warsaw (and Galicia after 1941), but excluding the western Polish provinces, which were annexed directly to Germany.

Genocide   Term coined by Raphael Lemkin in 1944 to refer to the destruction of a nation or ethnic group. The United Nations Genocide Convention of 1948 determined that genocide could occur through killing, torture, deprivation of adequate living conditions, or prevention of reproduction.

Gens, Jakob (1905–43)   Head of the ghetto administration in Wilno.

Ghetto   An urban area where Jews were compelled by law to reside. From the sixteenth to the eighteenth century ghettos were common in Italy and central Europe; the last such ghetto was dissolved in 1870. The Nazis revived the institution in occupied Poland and extended it to the Soviet territories conquered in 1941.

Globocnik, Odilo (1904–45)   SS and Police Leader of the Lublin district from November 1939; principal architect of Operation Reinhard.

Goering, Hermann (1893–46)   Principal Nazi leader after Hitler and Hitler's designated successor. Holding the title Reich Marshal, he was interior minister of Prussia, head of the German air force, plenipotentiary of the Four-Year Plan for economic revival, and minister of the economy.

Haavara (Hebrew: Transfer)   1933 agreement between the Nazi government and agencies of the Zionist movement allowing German Jews migrating to Palestine to transfer a portion of their assets with them.

Heydrich, Reinhard (1904–42)   Head of the RSHA, Protector of Bohemia and Moravia, and organizer of the *Einsatzgruppen*. Heydrich was one of the primary planners and executors of the Nazi mass murder campaign.

Himmler, Heinrich (1900–45)   Head of the SS; along with Hitler and Goering the most powerful leader of the Third Reich. He oversaw the planning and execution of the murder campaign, supervising the work of Heydrich and Eichmann.

Hitler Youth   Nazi organization for boys aged 15–18; membership was compulsory from 1936. Along with the League of German Girls, it provided a principal avenue of indoctrination for the Nazi regime.

Horthy, Miklos (1868–1957)   Regent of Hungary, 1920–44. Although he resisted German demands to turn responsibility for Hungarian Jews over to the SS, his withdrawal from active political involvement between March and July 1944 opened the way for 430,000 Jews to be deported.

Intentionalist/functionalist debate   Historiographical controversy concerning (among other things) the origins of the Holocaust. Intentionalists argue that systematic mass killing of Jews was Hitler's plan before he came to power; functionalists argue that the idea of mass killing evolved only after the invasion of the USSR in 1941.

Intergovernmental Committee on Refugees   Body established by the Evian Conference in 1938. In 1939 it negotiated an arrangement allowing German Jews leaving the country to take their assets with them. The arrangement was not implemented due to the outbreak of war. During the war it was largely inactive.

Jewish Agency for Palestine   Body created in 1929 to represent the Jewish community of Palestine in political matters. Though including non-Zionists, it was closely associated with the Zionist movement.

Jewish Fighting Organization   Armed resistance group established in Warsaw in July 1942; principal force behind the Warsaw ghetto revolt. Branches were established in Białystok, Kraków, and other ghettos as well.

Jewish reservation   Idea floated within the Nazi regime in 1939–40, involving mass concentration of Jews in a single location. Proposed locations were Nisko (Poland) and Madagascar.

Judenrat (pl. *Judenräte*)   Official Jewish administrations established at German behest in most east European ghettos and in several other occupied countries.

Karski, Jan (1914–)   Polish underground courier. In 1940 and 1942 he transmitted eyewitness testimony about the fate of Polish Jews to the Polish government-in-exile. In 1942–43 he also informed British and US leaders about the systematic mass murder of Europe's Jews.

Killing centres   Term referring to six German-established locations (Chełmno, Bełżec, Sobibór, Treblinka, Majdanek, and Birkenau) to which Jews were transported from across Europe to be killed.

Kovner, Abba (1918–87)   Leader of the United Partisan Organization in the Wilno ghetto. Kovner was the first Jew known to have deduced the German murder plan and the first to call for Jewish armed resistance.

Kristallnacht   Nazi-organized anti-Jewish riot of 9–10 November 1938, in which synagogues were burned and Jewish property looted throughout Germany and Austria.

Labour camps   Camps where a minority of young, healthy Jews were exploited, along with non-Jews, as forced labourers instead of being killed immediately.

Law for the Restoration of the Professional Civil Service   The first major piece of Nazi anti-Jewish legislation. Adopted in April 1933, it removed Jewish government employees from their positions.

Lemkin, Raphael (1901–59)   Polish Jewish refugee legal scholar who coined the term 'genocide' in 1944.

Madagascar Plan   Nazi plan to create a Jewish reservation on the east African island of Madagascar. Developed by the SS and the German foreign ministry, it received much attention within the Nazi regime in 1940, but it was abandoned late in the year, when the decision was taken to invade the Soviet Union.

Majdanek   Killing centre combined with concentration camp on the outskirts of Lublin. About 500,000 Jews, Poles, and Soviet prisoners were brought to the camp between October 1941 and July 1944; 150,000 Jews from many European countries were killed there in gas chambers.

Mein Kampf   Hitler's autobiography and main ideological tract, published 1925–28. Among other things, it is a principal source for the reconstruction of Hitler's ideas and plans concerning Jews.

Merin, Moshe (1906–43)   Head of the *Judenrat* in the Zagłębie region of Poland (eastern Upper Silesia), including the communities of Będzin and Sosnowiec.

Mischling (pl. *Mischlinge*)   Category defined in the wake of the Nuremberg Laws, consisting of people with one or two Jewish grandparents who did not adhere to the Jewish religion and were not married to Jews. Because of their 'mixed blood', they were subject to certain restrictions in marriage and employment, which increased in severity in accordance with the percentage of Jewishness in an individual's pedigree.

Nazi Party   Common name of the National Socialist German Workers Party, founded in 1919 (known as the German Workers Party until 1920). Led by Hitler, it became the largest German political party in the July 1932 parliamentary elections. In January 1933 it took control of the government with Hitler as Chancellor (premier); two months later it altered the German constitution and inaugurated the Third Reich.

Nisko Plan   Nazi scheme to create a Jewish reservation in the eastern Generalgouvernement, to which Jews from throughout the Nazi realm would be deported. Several tens of thousands of Jews were deported there from the Protectorate and western Poland in late 1939, but the operation was abandoned in early 1940 in favour of the Madagascar Plan.

Nuremberg Laws   Name for two German laws promulgated on 15 September 1935. The Reich Citizenship Law stated that only people with pure German blood could be German citizens; all others were classified as 'subjects'. The Law for the Protection of German Blood and Honour outlawed marriages between citizens and subjects. In November 1935 a third category, *Mischlinge*, was added.

Operation Reinhard   Codename for the construction of the Bełżec, Sobibór, and Treblinka killing centres and their use in the murder of over 2 million Jews from the Generalgouvernement.

Protectorate of Bohemia and Moravia   German administrative unit established in the Czech lands following the conquest of Czechoslovakia in March 1939. Though officially run by Czechs, sole political authority actually rested with the German Protector and his officials.

Regat   Area of Romania comprising the two original Romanian provinces of Moldavia and Wallachia, excluding outlying regions (including Bukovina, Bessarabia, and Transylvania) annexed from 1913 on. Despite German pressure, Romanian dictator Antonescu refused to turn Regat Jews over to the Germans for deportation.

Reich Labour Service   German government labour battalion to which German men and women aged 19–25 could be conscripted for six months. It served as an important indoctrinatory vehicle for the Nazi regime.

Reichsvereinigung and Reichsvertretung   Names of the central organizations of German Jewry under Nazi rule. The Reichsvertretung der deutschen Juden (Reich Representation of German Jews) was a voluntary social welfare organization; in 1935 it was ordered to change its name to the Reichsvertretung der Juden in Deutschland (Reich Representation of the Jews in Germany) – the Nuremberg Laws having made the term 'German Jews' untenable. In 1939 the Reichsvertretung was converted by government action into the Reichsvereinigung der Juden in Deutschland (Reich Association of the Jews in Germany); it became the legally recognized official administration of the German Jewish community and was charged with effectuating mass Jewish emigration.

'Resettlement in the east'   German euphemism for deportation of Jews to killing centres.

Ringelblum, Emmanuel (1900–1944)   Jewish historian and social worker from Warsaw. A leader of the Jewish self-help effort in the Warsaw ghetto, he established a clandestine information service and archive, which has become a principal source of information about how Jews in the ghetto lived under Nazi occupation. He was instrumental in gathering, collating, and transmitting information about mass murders of Jews.

RSHA   Acronym for Reichssicherheitshauptamt (Reich Main Security Office). Organized in September 1939 as a branch of the SS under Heydrich, the RSHA supervised the criminal police (Kripo), the secret political police (Gestapo), and the internal espionage service (SD).

Rumkowski, Mordechai Hayim (1877–1944)   'Eldest of the Jews' (head of the *Judenrat*) in the Łódź ghetto.

Salvation through work   Survival strategy employed by several *Judenrat* heads. It involved intensive Jewish-initiated exploitation of the industrial and labour resources of ghettos for German war production, in the hope that the Germans would regard Jews as too valuable to the German war effort to be killed.

Selection   Removal of young and healthy Jews from the ranks of those transported to killing centres, in order to exploit their labour or use them in medical experiments.

Sinti and Roma   The two largest European Gypsy groups, distinguished by language. Sinti were more numerous in Germany, Roma throughout Europe. The origins of both groups can be traced to India, and their presence was noted in Europe from the fifteenth century. There are many similarities between the treatment of Jews by the Third Reich and the treatment of Gypsies. Gypsies were victims of mass murder; estimates of the number killed range from 200,000 to 1,000,000.

Sobibór   German killing centre in eastern Poland. Some 250,000 Jews were killed in the Sobibór gas chambers between March 1942 and September 1943.

Sonderkommando   Name assigned to deportees selected upon arrival at killing centres to perform particularly gruesome duties associated with disposing of the bodies of the victims.

SS   Nazi police force and Hitler's personal bodyguard corps, transformed under Himmler's leadership into the principal police agency in the Third Reich. Its primary task under Himmler was to survey and eliminate all activity that might threaten the Reich. In this capacity it supervised most of the German concentration camps and took on primary responsibility for controlling (and eventually killing) the Jewish population in German-occupied territories.

T4   Code name for a Nazi programme to kill mentally retarded and physically deformed individuals believed to present a danger of corrupting German racial stock. Operating in 1939–41, it was responsible for the development of techniques (including mass killing by asphyxiation) that were later employed in the murder of Jews. Some T4 workers were instrumental in the initial operation of the killing centres.

Transnistria   Ukrainian region between the Bug and Dniester Rivers, occupied by Romania from 1941 to 1944. The Romanian government deported some 150,000 Jews, mostly from Bukovina and Bessarabia, to Transnistria, where they were incarcerated in ghettos and camps and conscripted for forced labour. About 90,000 of the deportees died. In addition, some 185,000 Jews who had lived in the region before the Romanian occupation were murdered by German and Romanian forces.

Treblinka   German killing centre midway between Warsaw and Białystok. About 870,000 Jews were killed there between July 1942 and July 1943, almost all from the Generalgouvernement.

Ustaše (Serbo-Croat: Insurgents)   Units of a right-wing Croatian nationalist separatist paramilitary organization, led by Ante Pavelić. They came to power with Germany's creation of an independent Croatian satellite in 1941 and without German assistance initiated mass killings of non-Croatians, including 500,000 Serbs, 35,000 Jews, and 20,000 Gypsies.

Volk (pl. *Völker*)   German word literally meaning 'people'. Hitler used it as a substitute for the term 'race', indicating a fundamental genetic division of humanity. *Völker*, in Hitler's view, were the repositories of all values.

Wallenberg, Raoul (1912–?)   Special representative sent by the Swedish Foreign Ministry and US War Refugee Board to Budapest in 1944 to offer protection to Hungarian Jews threatened with death. By distributing special Swedish passports and establishing special Jewish hostels, Wallenberg managed to prevent the deportation or shooting of perhaps as many as 100,000 Jews.

Wannsee Conference   Meeting held in Berlin in January 1942 to establish a timetable and coordinate the logistics of the transportation of European Jews to the killing centres.

War Refugee Board   US government agency established in January 1944 to explore possibilities for rescuing European Jews.

Weimar Republic   Name commonly used to designate the German republic established in February 1919. Fourteen years later it gave way to the Third Reich.

Yad Vashem   The official Israeli institution for studying and commemorating the Holocaust. Among other activities it maintains an extensive library and archive; it also honours and gathers information about non-Jews who risked their lives to assist Jews during the Holocaust.

Żegota   Codename for the Council for Aid to Jews, established under the aegis of the Polish underground in December 1942. It assisted some 4,000 Polish Jews to maintain themselves in hiding or under cover of false identity during the German occupation.

Zionism   Modern Jewish political and ideological movement arguing that Jews constitute primarily a national group (comparable to Germans or Poles) instead of a religious one (comparable to Catholics or Muslims) and that as such they are entitled to political sovereignty over their historic homeland. During the early twentieth century the World Zionist Organization, established in 1897, encouraged Jewish migration to Palestine, where, it hoped, a large Jewish settlement would serve as the basis for a Jewish national home. Zionism was a controversial idea among Jews from its inception; nonetheless, from the end of the First World War it was one of the principal forces in European Jewish life.

Zyklon B   Trade name of prussic acid or hydrogen cyanide (HCN), a lethal substance used in the gas chambers at Birkenau.

BIBLIOGRAPHY

PRIMARY SOURCES AND DOCUMENT COLLECTIONS

1 Adam, U.D., 'An overall plan for anti-Jewish legislation in the Third Reich?', *Yad Vashem Studies* 11 (1976): 33–55.

2 Arad, Y., Gutman, Y. and Margaliot, A. (eds), *Documents on the Holocaust: Selected Sources on the Destruction of the Jews of Germany and Austria, Poland, and the Soviet Union,* Yad Vashem, Jerusalem, 1981.

3 Blumenthal, N. (ed.), *Darko shel Judenrat: Te'udot miGeto Białystok* (Conduct and Actions of a Judenrat: Documents from the Białystok Ghetto), Yad Vashem, Jerusalem, 1962.

4 Borwicz, M., Rost, N. and Wulf, J. (eds), *Dokumenty zbrodni i męczeństwa* (Documents of Iniquity and Martyrdom), Regional Jewish Historical Commission, Kraków, 1945.

5 Burdick, C. and Jacobsen, H-A. (eds), *The Halder War Diary 1939–1942,* Presidio Press, Novato, CA, 1988.

6 Dawidowicz, L.S. (ed.), *A Holocaust Reader,* Behrman House, New York, 1976.

. 7 Heiber, H., 'Der Generalplan Ost', *Vierteljahrshefte für Zeitgeschichte* 6 (1958): 281–325.

8 Engel, D., 'An early account of Polish Jewry under Nazi and Soviet occupation presented to the Polish government-in-exile, February 1940', *Jewish Social Studies* 45 (1983): 1–16.

9 Engel, D., 'Moshe Kleinbaum's report on issues in the former eastern Polish territories, 12 March 1940', in N. Davies and A. Polonsky (eds), *Jews in Eastern Poland and the USSR, 1939–1946,* Macmillan, London, 1991, pp. 275–300.

10 Grynberg, M. (ed.), *Pamiętniki z getta warszawskiego* (Warsaw Ghetto Memoirs), PWN, Warsaw, 1993.

11 Hertz, J.S. (ed.), *Zygielbojm-Bukh* (Zygielbojm Book), Unser Tsait, New York, 1947.

12 Hilberg, R. (ed.), *Documents of Destruction: Germany and Jewry 1933–1945,* Quadrangle Books, Chicago, IL, 1971.

13   Hilberg, R., Staron, S. and Kermisz, J. (eds), *The Warsaw Diary of Adam Czerniaków: Prelude to Doom*, Stein and Day, New York, 1979.

14   Hitler, A., *Mein Kampf*, trans. Ralph Mannheim, Houghton Mifflin, Boston, MA, 1943.

15   Hitler, A., *Hitler's Secret Book*, trans. Salvator Attanasio, Grove Press, New York, 1961.

16   Karski, J., *Story of a Secret State*, Houghton Mifflin, Boston, MA, 1944.

17   Kellermann, H., 'Ende der Emanzipation?', *Der Morgen* 9 (August 1933): 173–7.

18   Kurczak, Różka, *Lehavot baEfer* (Flames in the Ash), Sifriat Poalim, Tel Aviv, 1965.

19   Lemkin, R., *Axis Rule in Occupied Europe: Laws of Occupation, Analysis of Government Proposals for Redress*, Carnegie Endowment for International Peace, Washington, DC, 1944.

20   Lemkin, R., 'My battle with half the world', *Chicago Jewish Forum*, Winter 1952.

21   Makower, H., *Pamiętnik z getta warszawskiego* (Memoir of the Warsaw Ghetto), Ossolineum, Wrocław, 1987.

22   Mendes-Flohr, P. and Reinharz, J. (eds), *The Jew in the Modern World: A Documentary History*, 2nd edn, Oxford University Press, New York, 1995.

23   Phelps, R.H., 'Hitlers "grundlegende" Rede über den Antisemitismus', *Vierteljahrshefte für Zeitgeschichte* 16 (1968): 390–420.

24   Prekerowa, T., *Konspiracyjna Rada Pomocy Żydom w Warszawie 1942–1945* (The Secret Council for Aid to Jews in Warsaw), Państwowy Instytut Wydawniczy, Warsaw, 1982.

25   Rauschning, H., *The Revolution of Nihilism: Warning to the West*, trans. W.E. Dickes, Longmans, Green & Co., New York, 1939.

26   Reichmann, E.G., *Größe und Verhängnis deutsch-jüdischer Existenz: Zeugnisse einer tragischen Begegnung* (The Greatness and Misfortune of German–Jewish Existence: Testimonials to a Tragic Encounter), Lambert Schneider, Heidelberg, 1974.

27   Richarz, M. (ed.), *Jewish Life in Germany: Memoirs from Three Centuries*, Indiana University Press, Bloomington, IN, 1991.

28   Shirer, W.L., *Berlin Diary*, Pocket Books, New York, 1941.

29   State of Israel, Ministry of Justice, *The Trial of Adolf Eichmann: Record of Proceedings in the District Court of Jerusalem*, Yad Vashem, Jerusalem, 1993.

30   *Trials of the Major War Criminals before the International Military Tribunal*, 42 vols, International Military Tribunal, Nuremberg, 1949.

31   *Trials of War Criminals before the Nuernberg Military Tribunals*, 18 vols, US Government Printing Office, Washington, 1952.

32   Trunk, I. (ed.), *Lodzher Getto* (The Łódź Ghetto), Marston Press, New York, 1962.

33   Zalzer, Maria (ed.), *Weg und Schicksal der Stuttgarter Juden* (Stuttgart Jews: Their Road and their Fate) Ernst Klett Verlag, Stuttgart, [1964].

SECONDARY SOURCES

34   Abel, T.F., *Why Hitler Came Into Power: An Answer based on the Original Life Stories of Six Hundred of his Followers*, Prentice-Hall, New York, 1938.

35   Abrahamsen, S., *Norway's Response to the Holocaust*, Holocaust Library, New York, 1991.

36   Adam, U.D., 'Nazi actions concerning the Jews between the beginning of World War II and the German attack on the USSR', in F. Furet (ed.), *Unanswered Questions: Nazi Germany and the Genocide of the Jews*, Schocken Books, New York, 1989, pp. 84–95.

37   Allen, W.S., *The Nazi Seizure of Power: The Experience of a Single German Town 1930–1935*, Eyre and Spottiswoode, London, 1966.

38   Aly, G. and Heim, S., *Vordenker der Vernichtung: Auschwitz und die deutschen Pläne für eine neue europäische Ordnung* (Pioneers of Destruction: Auschwitz and the German Plans for a New European Order), Fischer, Frankfurt am Main, 1993.

39   Arad, Y., *Belzec, Sobibor, Treblinka: The Operation Reinhard Death Camps*, Indiana University Press, Bloomingtom, IN, 1987.

40   Aschheim, S.E., 'Small forays, grand theories and deep origins: current trends in the historiography of the Holocaust', *Studies in Contemporary Jewry* 10 (1994): 139–63.

41   Ball-Kaduri, K.Y., 'The National Representation of Jews in Germany – obstacles and accomplishments at its establishment', *Yad Vashem Studies* 2 (1958): 159–78.

42   Bankier, D., *The Germans and the Final Solution: Public Opinion under Nazism*, Blackwell Publishers, Oxford, 1992.

43   Bankier, D., 'On modernization and the rationality of extermination', *Yad Vashem Studies* 24 (1994): 109–29.

44   Barkai, A., *From Boycott to Annihilation: The Economic Struggle of German Jews, 1933–1943*, University Press of New England, Hanover, NH, 1989.

45   Barkai, A., 'German interests in the Haavara-Transfer Agreement 1933–1939', *Leo Baeck Institute Year Book* 35 (1990): 245–66.

46   Bartoszewski, W., 'Polish-Jewish relations in occupied Poland, 1939–1945', in C. Abramsky, M. Jachimczyk and A. Polonsky (eds), *The Jews in Poland*, Basil Blackwell, Oxford, 1986, pp. 147–60.

47   Bartov, O., *Hitler's Army: Soldiers, Nazis, and War in the Third Reich*, Oxford University Press, New York, 1991.

48   Bartov, O., 'Ordinary monsters', *New Republic* 214: 18 (29 April 1996): 32–8.

49   Bar-Zohar, M., *Beyond Hitler's Grasp: The Heroic Rescue of Bulgaria's Jews*, Adams Media Corp., Holbrook, MA, 1998.

50   Bauer, Y., 'Gypsies', *Encyclopedia of the Holocaust*, Macmillan, New York, 1990.

51   Bauer, Y., 'Genocide: was it the Nazis' original plan?', *Annals of the American Academy of Political and Social Science* 450 (July 1980): 35–45.

52   Bauer, Y., *A History of the Holocaust*, Franklin Watts, New York, 1982.

53   Bauer, Y., *The Holocaust in Historical Perspective*, University of Washington Press, Seattle, WA, 1978.

54   Bauer, Y., *Jews for Sale? Nazi-Jewish Negotiations, 1933–1945*, Yale University Press, New Haven, CT, 1994.

55   Bauman, Z., *Modernity and the Holocaust*, Cornell University Press, Ithaca, NY, 1989.

56   Birn, R.B., 'Revising the Holocaust', *Historical Journal* 40:1 (1997): 195–209.

57   Bracher, K.D., *The German Dictatorship*, trans. Jean Steinberg, Praeger Publishers, New York, 1970.

58   Braham, R.L., *The Politics of Genocide: The Holocaust in Hungary*, Columbia University Press, New York, 1981.

59   Braham, R.L., 'The rightists, Horthy, and the Germans: factors underlying the destruction of Hungarian Jewry', in B. Vago and G. Mosse (eds), *Jews and Non-Jews in Eastern Europe*, John Wiley & Sons, New York, 1974, pp. 137–56.

60   Breitman, R.D., *The Architect of Genocide: Himmler and the Final Solution*, Brandeis University Press, Hanover, NH, 1991.

61   Breitman, R.D. and Kraut, A.M., *American Refugee Policy and European Jewry, 1933–1945*, Indiana University Press, Bloomington, IN, 1987.

62   Browning, C.R., 'Daniel Goldhagen's willing executioners', *History and Memory* 8:1 (1996): 88–108.

63   Browning, C.R., *The Final Solution and the German Foreign Office: A Study of Referat D III of Abteilung Deutschland 1940–43*, Holmes and Meier, New York, 1978.

64   Browning, C.R., *Ordinary Men: Reserve Police Battalion 101 and the Final Solution in Poland*, Harper Collins, New York, 1992.

65   Browning, C.R., *The Path to Genocide: Essays on Launching the Final Solution*, Cambridge University Press, Cambridge, 1992.

66   Broszat, M., 'Hitler and the genesis of the "final solution": an assessment of David Irving's theses', *Yad Vashem Studies* 13 (1979): 73–125.

67   Broszat, M., 'A plea for the historicization of National Socialism', in P. Baldwin (ed.), *Reworking the Past: Hitler, the Holocaust, and the Historian's Debate*, Beacon Press, Boston, 1990.

68   Brustein, W., *The Logic of Evil: The Social Origins of the Nazi Party, 1925–1933*, Yale University Press, New Haven, CT, 1996.

69   Burleigh, M. and Wippermann, W., *The Racial State: Germany 1933–1945*, Cambridge University Press, Cambridge, 1991.

70   Burrin, P., *Hitler and the Jews: The Genesis of the Holocaust*, Edward Arnold, London, 1994.

71   Chary, F., *The Bulgarian Jews and the Final Solution, 1940–1944*, University of Pittsburgh Press, Pittsburgh, PA, 1972.

72   Chazan, R., *In the Year 1096 ...*, Jewish Publication Society of America, Philadelphia, PA, 1996.

73   Cohen, J., *The Friars and the Jews: The Evolution of Medieval Anti-Judaism*, Cornell University Press, Ithaca, NY, 1982.

74   Cohen, M.J., *Palestine: Retreat from the Mandate: The Making of British Policy, 1936–1945*, Frank Cass, London, 1978.

75   Colodner, S., *Jewish Education in Germany under the Nazis*, Jewish Education Committee Press, New York, 1964.

76   *The Jews of Czechoslovakia*, 3 vols, Jewish Publication Society of America, Philadelphia, PA, 1968–.

77   Dawidowicz, L.S., *The War Against the Jews 1933–1945*, Holt, Rinehart and Winston, New York, 1975.

78   Diner, D., 'Rationalization and method: critique of a new approach in understanding the "final solution"', *Yad Vashem Studies* 24 (1994): 71–108.

79   Engel, D., *Facing a Holocaust: The Polish Government-in-Exile and the Jews, 1943–1945*, University of North Carolina Press, Chapel Hill, NC, 1993.

80   Engel, D., *In the Shadow of Auschwitz: The Polish Government-in-Exile and the Jews, 1939–1942*, University of North Carolina Press, Chapel Hill, NC, 1987.

81   Engel, D., 'Jan Karski's mission to the West', *Holocaust and Genocide Studies* 5 (1990): 363–80.

82   Engel, D., 'The Western Allies and the Holocaust', *Polin* 1 (1986): 300–16.

83   Engel, D., '"Will they dare?" Perceptions of threat in Jewish diaries from the Warsaw ghetto', in press.

84   Esh, Sh., *Iyyunim beHeker haSho'ah veYahadut Zemanenu* (Studies in the Holocaust and Contemporary Jewry), Institute of Contemporary Jewry, Jerusalem, 1979.

85   Fein, H., *Accounting for Genocide: National Responses and Jewish Victimization during the Holocaust*, University of Chicago Press, Chicago, 1979.

86   Feingold, H., *The Politics of Rescue: The Roosevelt Administration and the Holocaust, 1938–1945*, Rutgers University Press, New Brunswick, NJ, 1970.

87   Ferencz, B., *Less than Slaves: Jewish Forced Labor and the Quest for Compensation*, Harvard University Press, Cambridge, MA, 1979.

88   Fleming, G., *Hitler and the Final Solution*, University of California Press, Berkeley, CA, 1984.

89   Friedlander, H., *The Origins of Nazi Genocide: From Euthanasia to the Final Solution*, University of North Carolina Press, Chapel Hill, NC, 1995.

90   Friedländer, S., *L'antisémitisme nazi: histoire d'une psychose collective*, Éditions du Seuil, Paris, 1971.

91   Friedländer, S., *Memory, History, and the Extermination of the Jews of Europe*, Indiana University Press, Bloomington, IN, 1992.

92   Friedländer, S., *Nazi Germany and the Jews*, vol. 1, *The Years of Persecution*, Harper Collins, New York, 1997.

93   Friedländer, S., 'On the possibility of the Holocaust: an approach to a historical synthesis', in Y. Bauer and N. Rotenstreich (eds), *The Holocaust as Historical Experience*, Holmes and Meier, New York, 1981, pp. 1–21.

94   Friedländer, S., *Probing the Limits of Representation: National Socialism and the 'Final Solution'*, Harvard University Press, Cambridge, MA, 1992.

95   Friedman, P., *Roads to Extinction: Essays on the Holocaust*, Conference on Jewish Social Studies, New York, 1980.

96   Friedman, S.S., *No Haven for the Oppressed: United States Policy Toward Jewish Refugees, 1938–1945*, Wayne State University Press, Detroit, MI, 1973.

97   Fritz, S.G., *Frontsoldaten: The German Soldier in World War II*, University Press of Kentucky, Lexington, KY, 1995.

98   Funkenstein, A., 'Theological interpretations of the Holocaust: a balance', in F. Furet (ed.), *Unanswered Questions: Nazi Germany and the Genocide of the Jews*, Schocken Books, New York, 1989, pp. 275–303.

99   Gilbert, M., *Auschwitz and the Allies*, Holt, Rinehart and Winston, New York, 1981.

100   Goldhagen, D.J., *Hitler's Willing Executioners: Ordinary Germans and the Holocaust*, A.E. Knopf, New York, 1996.

101   Goodrick-Clarke, N., *The Occult Roots of Nazism: Secret Aryan Cults and Their Influence on Nazi Ideology*, New York University Press, New York, 1992

102   Gordon, S., *Hitler, Germans, and the 'Jewish Question'*, Princeton University Press, Princeton, NJ, 1984.

103   Gottlieb, M.R., *American Anti-Nazi Resistance 1933–1941*, Ktav Publishers, New York, 1982.

104   Gutman, I., *The Jews of Warsaw: Ghetto, Underground, Revolt*, Indiana University Press, Bloomington, IN, 1982.

105   Gutman, I., 'Youth movements in the underground and the ghetto revolts', in *Jewish Resistance during the Holocaust*, Yad Vashem, Jerusalem, 1971, pp. 260–81.

106   Gutman, I. and Krakowski, S., *Unequal Victims: Poles and Jews during World War II*, Holocaust Library, New York, 1986.

107 Heilbronner, O., 'The role of Nazi antisemitism in the Nazi party's activity and propaganda: a regional historiographical study', *Leo Baeck Institute Year Book* 35 (1990): 397–439.

108 Heim, S., and Aly, G., 'The holocaust and population policy: remarks on the decision on the "final solution"', *Yad Vashem Studies* 24 (1994): 45–70.

109 Heller, C.S., *On the Edge of Destruction: Jews of Poland between the Two World Wars*, Columbia University Press, New York, 1977.

110 Herbert, U., 'Racism and rational calculation: the role of "utilitarian" strategies of legitimation in the National Socialist "Weltanschauung"', *Yad Vashem Studies* 24 (1994): 131–45.

111 Hilberg, R., *The Destruction of the European Jews*, Holmes and Meier, New York, 1985.

112 Hilberg, R., *Perpetrators, Victims, Bystanders*, Aaron Asher Books, New York, 1992.

113 Hillgruber, A., *Germany and the Two World Wars*, trans. W.C. Kirby, Harvard University Press, Cambridge, MA, 1981.

114 Israel, J.I., *European Jewry in the Age of Mercantilism 1550–1750*, 2nd edn, Clarendon Press, Oxford, 1989.

115 Jäckel, E., *Hitler in History*, Brandeis University Press, Hanover, NH, 1984.

116 Jäckel, E., *Hitler's World View: A Blueprint for Power*, trans. Herbert Arnold, Harvard University Press, Cambridge, MA, 1981.

117 Kaplan, M., *Between Dignity and Despair: Jewish Life in Nazi Germany*, Oxford University Press, Oxford, 1998.

118 Katz, J., *From Prejudice to Destruction: Anti-Semitism 1700–1933*, Harvard University Press, Cambridge, MA, 1980.

119 Katz, J., 'Was the Holocaust predictable?' *Commentary*, May 1975.

120 Katz, S.T., *The Holocaust in Historical Context*, vol. 1, *The Holocaust and Mass Death Before the Modern Age*, Oxford University Press, New York, 1994.

121 Ka-Tzetnik 135633 [=Yehiel De-Nur], *Shivitti: A Vision*, Harper & Row, San Francisco, 1989.

122 Kershaw, I., *The 'Hitler Myth': Image and Reality in the Third Reich*, Oxford University Press, Oxford, 1987.

123 Kershaw, I., *The Nazi Dictatorship: Problems and Perspectives of Interpretation*, Edward Arnold, London, 1985.

124 Kershaw, I., 'The persecution of the Jews and German popular opinion in the Third Reich', *Leo Baeck Institute Year Book* 26 (1981): 261–89.

125 Korboński, S., *The Polish Underground State: A Guide to the Underground 1939–1945*, Columbia University Press, New York, 1978.

126 Krakowski, S., *The War of the Doomed: Jewish Armed Resistance in Poland, 1942–1944*, Holmes and Meier, New York, 1984.

127 Kramer, D., 'Jewish welfare work under the impact of pauperisation', in A. Paucker (ed.), *The Jews in Nazi Germany 1933–1943*, J.C.B. Mohr, Tübingen, 1986, pp. 173–88.

128   Krausnick, H., 'The persecution of the Jews', in *Anatomy of the SS State*, Walker, New York, 1968, pp. 1–124.

129   Kulka, O.D., 'Public opinion in Nazi Germany and the "Jewish question"', *Jerusalem Quarterly* 25 (Fall 1982): 121–44.

130   Lamberti, M., 'The Jewish defence in Germany after the National-Socialist seizure of power', *Leo Baeck Institute Year Book* 42 (1997): 135–47.

131   Langmuir, G., *Toward a Definition of Antisemitism*, University of California Press, Berkeley, CA, 1990.

132   Laqueur, W., *The Terrible Secret: Suppression of the Truth about Hitler's 'Final Solution'*, Little, Brown, and Company, Boston, 1980.

133   Lavi, T., 'The background to the rescue of Romanian Jewry during the period of the Holocaust', in B. Vago and G. Mosse (eds), *Jews and Non-Jews in Eastern Europe*, John Wiley & Sons, New York, 1974, pp. 177–86.

134   Lavsky, H., *Before Catastrophe: The Distinctive Path of German Zionism*, Wayne State University Press, Detroit, MI, 1996.

135   Levin, N., *The Holocaust: The Destruction of European Jewry 1933–1945*, Schocken Books, New York, 1973.

136   Levy, R.S., *The Downfall of the Anti-Semitic Political Parties in Imperial Germany*, Yale University Press, New Haven, CT, 1975.

137   Loewenberg, P., *Decoding the Past: The Psychohistorical Approach*, University of California Press, Berkeley and Los Angeles, CA, 1984.

138   Lukas, R.C., *The Forgotten Holocaust: The Poles under German Occupation 1939–1944*, University Press of Kentucky, Lexington, KY, 1986.

139   Margaliot, A., 'Emigration – Planung und Wirklichkeit', in A. Paucker (ed.), *The Jews in Nazi Germany 1933–1943*, J.C.B. Mohr, Tübingen, 1986, pp. 303–16.

140   Margaliot, A., 'The struggle for survival of the Jewish community in Germany in the face of oppression', in *Jewish Resistance during the Holocaust*, Yad Vashem, Jerusalem, 1971, pp. 100–11.

141   Marrus, M.R., *The Holocaust in History*, University Press of New England, Hanover, NH, 1987.

142   Marrus, M.R., *The Unwanted: European Refugees in the Twentieth Century*, Oxford University Press, Oxford, 1985.

143   Marrus, M.R. and Paxton, R.O., *Vichy France and the Jews*, Basic Books, New York, 1981.

144   Melzer, E., *No Way Out: The Politics of Polish Jewry, 1935–1939*, Hebrew Union College Press, Cincinnati, OH, 1997.

145   Mendelsohn, E., *The Jews of East Central Europe Between the World Wars*, Indiana University Press, Bloomington, IN, 1983.

146   Merkl, P., *Political Violence under the Swastika: 581 Early Nazis*, Princeton University Press, Princeton, NJ, 1975.

147   Michaelis, M., *Mussolini and the Jews: German–Italian Relations and the Jewish Question in Italy, 1922–1945*, Clarendon Press, Oxford, 1978.

148 Mommsen, H., 'The realization of the unthinkable: the "Final Solution of the Jewish Question" in the Third Reich', in G. Hirschfeld (ed.), *The Policies of Genocide: Jews and Soviet Prisoners of War in Nazi Germany*, Allen & Unwin, London, 1986.

149 Morgenthau, H., *The Tragedy of German-Jewish Liberalism*, Leo Baeck Memorial Lecture 4, Leo Baeck Institute, New York, 1961.

150 Mosse, G., *The Crisis of German Ideology: Intellectual Origins of the Third Reich*, Grosset and Dunlap, New York, 1964.

151 Mosse, G., *Toward the Final Solution: A History of European Racism*, Howard Fertig, New York, 1978.

152 Mosse, W.E. (ed.), *Deutsches Judentum in Krieg und Revolution 1916– 1923* (German Jewry in War and Revolution 1916–1923), J.C.B. Mohr, Tübingen, 1971.

153 Neumann, F., *Behemoth: The Structure and Practice of National Socialism 1933–1944*, Oxford University Press, New York, 1944.

154 Nicosia, F.R., *The Third Reich and the Palestine Question*, University of Texas Press, Austin, TX, 1985.

155 Niewyk, D.L., *The Jews in Weimar Germany*, Louisiana State University Press, Baton Rouge, LA, 1980.

156 Niewyk, D.L., 'Self-defence and German-Jewish identities', *Leo Baeck Institute Year Book* 42 (1997): 149–53.

157 Niewyk, D.L., *Socialist, Anti-Semite, and Jew: German Social Democracy Confronts the Problem of Anti-Semitism, 1918–1933*, Louisiana State University Press, Baton Rouge, LA, 1971.

158 Nolte, E., *Three Faces of Fascism: Action Francaise, Italian Fascism, National Socialism*, trans. Leila Vennewitz, Holt, Rinehart and Winston, New York, 1965.

159 Peled (Margolin), Y., *Krakov haYehudit 1939–1943* (Jewish Kraków 1939–1943), Hakibbutz Hameuchad, Tel Aviv, 1993.

160 Pingel, F., 'The concentration camps as part of the National Socialist system of domination', in Y. Gutman (ed.), *The Nazi Concentration Camps*, Yad Vashem, Jerusalem, 1984, pp. 3–17.

161 Poliakov, L., *Harvest of Hate: The Nazi Program for the Destruction of the Jews of Europe*, Jewish Publication Society of America, Philadelphia, PA, 1954.

162 Prekerowa, T., 'The Relief Council for Jews in Poland, 1942–1945', in C. Abramsky, M. Jachimczyk and A. Polonsky (eds), *The Jews in Poland*, Basil Blackwell, Oxford, 1986, pp. 161–76.

163 Pridham, G., *Hitler's Rise to Power: The Nazi Movement in Bavaria, 1923–1933*, Harper and Row, New York, 1973.

164 Rautkallio, H., *Finland and the Holocaust: The Rescue of Finland's Jews*, Holocaust Library, New York, 1987.

165 Rose, P.L., *German Question / Jewish Question: Revolutionary Antisemitism from Kant to Wagner*, Princeton University Press, Princeton, NJ, 1990.

166 Rosenbaum, A.S. (ed.), *Is the Holocaust Unique? Perspectives on Comparative Genocide*, Westview Press, Oxford, 1996.

167 Rubenstein, R.L. and Roth, J.K., *Approaches to Auschwitz: The Holocaust and its Legacy*, John Knox Press, Atlanta, GA, 1987.

168 Rubinstein, W.D., *The Myth of Rescue*, Routledge, London, 1997.

169 Ruether, R., *Faith and Fratricide: The Theological Roots of Anti-Semitism*, Seabury Press, New York, 1979.

170 Schleunes, K., 'Retracing the twisted road: Nazi policies toward German Jews, 1933–1939', in F. Furet (ed.), *Unanswered Questions: Nazi Germany and the Genocide of the Jews*, Schocken Books, New York, 1989, pp. 54–70.

171 Schleunes, K., *The Twisted Road to Auschwitz: Nazi Policy toward German Jews 1933–1939*, University of Illinois Press, Urbana, IL, 1970.

172 Sherman, A.J., *Island Refuge: Britain and Refugees from the Third Reich 1933–1939*, California University Press, Berkeley, CA, 1973.

173 Silberklang, D., 'The Allies and the Holocaust: a reappraisal', *Yad Vashem Studies* 24 (1994): 147–76.

174 Stannard, D., *American Holocaust: Columbus and the Conquest of the New World*, Oxford University Press, New York, 1992.

175 Steinberg, J., 'Types of genocide? Croations, Serbs, and Jews, 1941–5', in D. Cesarani (ed.), *The Final Solution: Origins and Implementation*, Routledge, London, 1994, pp. 175–93.

176 Strauss, H.A., 'Jewish emigration from Germany: Nazi policies and Jewish responses (I)', *Leo Baeck Institute Year Book* 25 (1980): 313–61.

177 Strauss, H.A., 'Jewish emigration from Germany: Nazi policies and Jewish responses (II)', *Leo Baeck Institute Year Book* 26 (1981): 343–409.

178 Streit, C., 'The German army and the politics of genocide', in G. Hirschfeld (ed.), *The Policies of Genocide: Jews and Soviet Prisoners of War in Nazi Germany*, Allen & Unwin, London, 1986, pp. 1–14.

179 Synan, E.A., *The Popes and the Jews in the Middle Ages*, Macmillan, New York, 1965.

180 Tal, U., 'On the study of the Holocaust and genocide,' *Yad Vashem Studies* 13 (1979): 7–52.

181 Tec, N., *When Light Pierced the Darkness: Christian Rescue of Jews in Nazi-Occupied Poland*, Oxford University Press, Oxford, 1986.

182 Tenenbaum, J., 'The Anti-Nazi Boycott Movement in the United States', *Yad Vashem Studies* 3 (1959): 141–59.

183 Toury, J., 'From forced emigration to expulsion – the Jewish exodus over the non-Slavic borders of the Reich as a prelude to the "final solution"', *Yad Vashem Studies* 17 (1986): 51–91.

184 Trunk, I., *Judenrat: The Jewish Councils in Eastern Europe under Nazi Occupation*, Macmillan, New York, 1972.

185   Vago, B., 'The reaction to the Nazi anti-Jewish policy in East-Central Europe and in the Balkans', in F. Furet (ed.), *Unanswered Questions: Nazi Germany and the Genocide of the Jews*, Schocken Books, New York, 1989, pp. 199–234.

186   Vago, B. and Mosse, G. (eds), *Jews and Non-Jews in Eastern Europe*, John Wiley & Sons, New York, 1974.

187   Wasserstein, B., *Britain and the Jews of Europe 1939–1945*, Oxford University Press, Oxford, 1979.

188   Weiss, A., 'Categories of camps – their character and role in the execution of the "final solution of the Jewish question"', in Y. Gutman (ed.), *The Nazi Concentration Camps*, Yad Vashem, Jerusalem, 1984, pp. 115–32.

189   Weiss, A., 'Jewish-Ukrainian relations in Western Ukraine during the Holocaust', in P.J. Potichnyj and H. Aster (eds), *Ukrainian-Jewish Relations in Historical Perspective*, Canadian Institute of Ukrainian Studies, Edmonton, 1988, pp. 409–20.

190   Weiss, J., *Ideology of Death: Why the Holocaust Happened in Germany*, Ivan R. Dee, Chicago, IL, 1996.

191   Weiss, Y., 'The Transfer Agreement and the Boycott Movement: a Jewish dilemma on the eve of the Holocaust', *Yad Vashem Studies* 26 (1998): 129–71.

192   Wood, E.T. and Jankowski, St., *Karski: How One Man Tried to Stop the Holocaust*, John Wiley, New York, 1994.

193   Wyman, D., *The Abandonment of the Jews: America and the Holocaust 1941–1945*, Pantheon Books, New York, 1984.

194   Wyman, D., *Paper Walls: America and the Refugee Crisis 1938–1941*, University of Massachusetts Press, Amherst, MA, 1968.

195   Yahil, L., *The Holocaust: The Fate of European Jewry, 1932–1945*, trans. I. Friedman and H. Galai, Oxford University Press, New York, 1990.

196   Yahil, L., 'Madagascar – phantom of a solution for the Jewish question', in B. Vago and G. Mosse (eds), *Jews and Non-Jews in Eastern Europe*, John Wiley & Sons, New York, 1974, pp. 315–34.

197   Yahil, L., *The Rescue of Danish Jewry: Test of a Democracy*, Jewish Publication Society of America, Philadelphia, PA, 1969.

198   Zucotti, S., *The Italians and the Holocaust: Persecution, Rescue, Survival*, Basic Books, New York, 1987.

Map 1   Europe and its Jews, January 1938

Map 2 *German, Hungarian, and Soviet expansion and the dismemberment of Czechoslovakia and Poland, 1938–39*

Map 3   The Nazi orbit, 1942

Map 4 The murder of European Jewry

INDEX

Africa, 31, 50, 59
Aktion, 60; in Lwów, 99
Allen, W.S., 21
Allied governments: asked to assist
  Jews, 105; and killing of Jews,
  77–80; see also Great Britain,
  United States
Ältestenrat, Ältestenrate, see
  Judenrat, Judenräte
Aly, Götz, 56
Americas, indigenous population
  of, 2
antisemites, antisemitism, 12;
  'eliminationist' (Goldhagen), 14;
  'redemptive' (Friedländer), 17
Antonescu, Ion, 73
Arabs, Palestinian, 47–8
Arlosoroff, Chaim, 45, 94
Armenians, 3
Army, German, 25, 57; Jews
  excluded from, 39
Arrow Cross, 74
Ashkenaz, Ashkenazic, see Jews
'asocials', 55, 58
Association des Juifs en Belgique,
  66
Auschwitz, 57, 81, 85; called
  'another planet', 5; demand
  to bomb, 78–9; see also
  Birkenau
Austria, 1, 35, 48, 50, 60;
  annexation of, 36, 41
Axis, 55

Baltic states, 35, 60, 71, 75; see
  also Estonia; Latvia; Lithuania
banks, 39
Barash, Efraim, 68; speaks to
  Białystok ghetto, 106–7
Bauer, Yehuda, 32, 62
Bauman, Zygmunt, 4, 85–6
Bavaria, 20
Becker, Rudolf, 29
Belgium, 1, 59, 66; armed
  resistance in, 71; opposition to
  deportation of Jews in, 72; takes
  in St Louis refugees, 49; see also
  Benelux countries
Bełżec, 57, 58, 60; eyewitness
  description of, 99–100; Jews in
  Warsaw learn about, 65
Benelux countries, 35; see also
  Belgium; Luxembourg; Netherlands
Berlin, 53; Jews deported from, 54
Bermuda Conference, 78
Bessarabia, 73, 74
Białystok, 103; ghetto liquidated,
  60; Judenrat, 68, 106–7
Birkenau, 57, 58, 81, 85; medical
  experiments at, 59; see also
  Auschwitz
Bohemia and Moravia, Protectorate
  of, 50, 53, 60; see also
  Czechoslovakia
Bolshevism, 36; Jews associated
  with, 13, 22, 53; see also
  communism, communists

Borki, 98
boycott: of Germany by Jews, 46;
   of Jewish businesses, 34
Breitman, Richard, 55
Broszat, Martin, 26, 28, 53, 54
Browning, Christopher, 23, 24, 53,
   55, 56
Brzeżany, 104
Buber, Martin, 44
Buchenwald, 58, 81
Budapest, 74, 79
Bug River, 73
Bukovina, Northern, 73, 74
Bulgaria, 1, 35, 60, 76; opposition
   to deportation of Jews in, 72
Bund report (May 1942), 65, 78,
   104–5
bureaucracy, 32, 85–6
Burleigh, Michael, 55
Burrin, Philippe, 55

Central Committee for Aid and
   Reconstruction, 42, 44
Central Office for Adult Jewish
   Education, 44
Central Office for Jewish
   Emigration, 36, 51
Chełmno, 57, 58, 104; news
   about, 65
Christian attitudes towards Jews,
   8–10
communism, communists, 39, 52,
   53; in Serbia, 60; see also
   Bolshevism
concentration camps, 39, 42, 81;
   distinguished from killing
   centres, 58
Copenhagen, 72
Council for Aid to Jews, see
   Żegota
courts, German, 39
Croatia, 35, 60, 76; deportation of
   Jews from, 73; see also
   Yugoslavia
Cromwell, Oliver, 11
crusades, 9

Cuba, 49
Czechoslovakia, 1, 35, 36, 48, 50;
   loses territory to Hungary, 74;
   see also Bohemia and Moravia,
   Protectorate of; Slovakia
Czerniaków, Adam, 67–8, 69;
   comments on suicide of, 108
Częstochowa, 60

Dachau, 58, 81
Danzig, 18
Dawidowicz, Lucy, 14; on Jewish
   reservation scheme, 31–2
death marches, 81
definitions of Jews, Nazi, 32–3
Denmark, 1, 59; Jews rescued in,
   72
De-Nur, Yehiel, 5, 84–5
Department of Racial Policy, 19
deportation of Jews, 53, 54; from
   France, 60; from General-
   gouvernement, 60, 61; from
   Slovakia, 60; from various
   European countries, 59
diaspora, 7, 8
Diels, Rudolf, 29
doctors, Jewish, 33

Economic Affairs Ministry,
   German, 45
Edict of Toleration, 11
education, Jewish, 43, 44
Edward I (of England), 10
Eichmann, Adolf, 19, 51, 59
Einsatzgruppen, 51, 57, 73, 75,
   86; shootings by described, 57,
   98–9, 102
Eisner, Kurt, 22
Elbe River, 11
emancipation, Jewish, 11
emigration, Jewish: obstacles to,
   41–4; as policy of Third Reich,
   30, 36, 37, 54; reverse, 42; sta-
   tistics, 41, 42; see also extrusion
Endziel, see 'final aim'

England, 10, 11, 12; *see also* Great Britain
Estonia, 1, 57; local volunteers assist *Einsatzgruppen* in, 75; *see also* Baltic states
Europe, Eastern: attitudes towards Jews in, 13; Jews in, 12
Evian Conference, 48
express letter (Heydrich), 30, 34
expropriation of Jewish property, 33
extrusion of Jews, 49-51; *see also* emigration

Fein, Helen, 76, 80
Feuchtwanger, Lion, 40
'final aim', 31
'final solution', 54, 56, 57, 96
Finland, 1, 59; opposition to deportation of Jews in, 72
First World War, 12, 36, 67, 82; and German attitudes towards Jews, 22
flight tax, 41, 43, 47
forced labour: by Hungarian Jews, 74; by Polish Jews, 67, 105–6; by Romanian Jews, 73
foreign ministry, German: memorandum on Jewish policy (1939), 30, 36, 37
Four-Year Plan, 36
France, 1, 10, 11, 12, 35, 36, 50, 51, 59, 66, 76; armed resistance in, 71; deportation of Jews from, 60, 72; Italian-occupied regions of, 72; takes in *St Louis* refugees, 49
Frank, Anne, 77
Frank, Hans, 63, 95; and Jews, 19; orders Jews to wear Star of David, 34; and Slavs, 19, 20
Frankfurter, Felix, 62–3
Friedlander, Henry, 55
Friedländer, Saul, 17, 22, 26, 81–2, 83–4

Functionalists, 27–8; and anti-Jewish violence, 34–5; and Heydrich express letter, 31; and transition to killing, 52–4
Funkenstein, Amos, 84

Galicia, 104
gas chambers, 58, 59, 104
gas vans, 58
Generalgouvernement, 19, 50, 63, 65, 70, 104; deportation of Jews from, 80
genocide, 2, 3, 19; defined, 88–9
Gens, Jakob, 68, 70
German Zionist Federation, 45
Germanic lands, 9, 10
Germans: and Jews, 20–1, 22
Germany, 1, 12, 14, 22, 36, 48, 50, 55, 60; attitudes towards Jews in, 18, 20–2; invades Poland, 49; invades Soviet Union, 52, 73; occupies Hungary, 74; position of Jews in, 13; prohibits Jews from leaving occupied areas, 51
Gestapo, 29
ghettos, 61, 63, 75; conditions in, 52, 95; in early modern Europe, 10; liquidation of, 60; Nazi policy regarding, 53; in occupied Poland, 34, 52, 53; in occupied Soviet Union, 53
Globocnik, Odilo, 60
Goebbels, Josef, 90
Goering, Hermann, 46, 54; and Jews, 19; orders 'final solution', 96
Goldhagen, Daniel, 14, 24, 25
Great Britain, 36, 47, 50, 51; limits Jewish immigration to Palestine, 48; takes in *St Louis* refugees, 49; *see also* Allied governments
Greece, 1, 35, 60, 66; Italian-occupied regions of, 72

Gypsies, 1, 2, 55; killed at Chełmno, 104; *see also* Roma; Sinti

Haavara (Transfer), 45–7, 48
Hamburg, Jews deported from, 54
handicapped, 55
Havana, 49
Hebrew, 10
Heim, Susanne, 56
Heydrich, Reinhard, 30–1, 54, 56, 57, 59, 60; issues invitation to Wannsee Conference, 97; receives order for 'final solution', 96
hiding of Jews, 77, 109; and betrayal, 71, 77, 110
Hilberg, Raul, 23, 32, 34, 35, 85
Himmler, Heinrich, 59, 60; and Jews, 19; and Poznań speech, 83, 110
'historicization', 26
Hitler, Adolf, 14, 18, 28, 35, 52, 54; on Jews, 14–17, 22–3, 29, 31, 40, 52, 89–90, 91; appointed German Chancellor, 39; associates Jews with Marxism, 22–3, 52; on black races, 17; discusses Jews with Horthy, 19, 91; foreign policy of, 36; intentionalist and functionalist appraisals of, 27; on Soviet Jews, 52; and theory of history, 15–16; threatens Jews in Reichstag speech, 31, 37
Hitler Youth, 25
Holland, *see* Netherlands
Holocaust: debate over 'uniqueness' of, 2–3; German people and, 21, 24; notable characteristics of, 83; use of term, 2, 5
homosexuals, 2, 55
Horthy, Miklos, 74, 79; discusses Jews with Hitler, 19, 91

Hungary, 1, 19, 35, 60, 66, 76, 79; Jews in, 13; and killing of Jews, 74; occupied by Germany, 74; proposal to ransom Jews in, 78–9

Iaşi, 73
immigration, Jewish, 47–9; to Palestine, 47–8
'indirect extermination', 62
Intentionalists, 27–8; and anti-Jewish violence, 34; and Heydrich express letter, 31; and transition to killing, 51–2
Intergovernmental Committee on Refugees, 48
intermarriage, Jewish–German, 13, 30; outlawed, 21, 33
Italy, 1, 10, 35, 59; aid to Jews in, 72; areas occupied by, 72; Jews escape through, 51

Jäckel, Eberhard, 36
Janowska, 59
Japan, 51
Jehovah's Witnesses, 2
Jewish Agency for Palestine, 45
Jewish Cultural Association, 42–3
Jewish Fighting Organization, 71, 76
Jewish reservation, 30, 31, 50
Jews: in the ancient world, 8; Ashkenazic, 8, 9, 10; Austrian, 48; businesses boycotted, 34; children dismissed from schools, 33; Czech, 48; defined by Nazis, 32–3; dismissed from jobs in Germany, 21, 33; distinguished from Poles by Nazis, 20; distinguishing characteristics of, 10; in Eastern Europe, 11–12, 47, 52–4, 57, 63–71; economic activities of, 9; economic conditions under Nazi rule, 39; eliminated from German civil service, 32; emancipation of, 11; emigrate from

Germany, 36; expelled from Reich, 50–1; as factor in Nazi foreign policy, 36–7; forced to assume special names, 33; in German public opinion, 20–1; in Germany, 13, 38–47; in Hitler's world-view, 14–17, 52; in Hungary, 13, 74; meanings of name, 7, 8; medieval expulsions of, 10; in Middle Ages, 9–10; in modern Europe, 10–13; in Nazi Party programme, 28; organize welfare under Nazis, 42–3; origins of, 7; in Poland, 12, 49, 52–4, 63–71; portrayed as parasites, 15–17, 28, 82, 89–90; property expropriated, 33; Reform, 11; religious outlook of, 8; in Romania, 13, 49, 73–4; in the Russian Empire, 11–12; Sefardic, 9; settle in Europe, 8; in the Soviet Union, 13, 53, 54, 57, 66; in United States, 12

Joodse Raad, 66
Joseph II (of Austria), 11
Judah, Judea, 7, 8
Judenrat, Judenräte, 29, 66–70, 105–8

Ka-Tzetnik, *see* De-Nur, Yehiel
Kaplan, Marion, 42
Karski, Jan, 62–3, 78; assesses conditions for Polish Jews, 101–2
Katz, Jacob, 41
Kaunas, 54, 69, 70, 104
Keitel, Wilhelm, 52
Kiev, 57
killing centres, 51, 57–9; distinguished from concentration camps, 58; liquidation of, 81; methods of killing in, 58; news about, 65
Kleinbaum, Moshe, 63–4
Kovner, Abba, 64–5, 70, 103

Kraków: armed resistance in, 71; liquidation of ghetto in, 60;
Kristallnacht, 21, 34, 42

labour camps, 59, 81
Laqueur, Walter, 79
Latin America, 49
Latvia, 1, 57; and assistance to *Einsatzgruppen*, 75; *see also* Baltic states; Riga
Law for the Protection of German Blood and Honour (1935), 32, 33; see *also* intermarriage; Nuremberg Laws
Law for the Restoration of the Professional Civil Service (1933), 32
Law on Reich Citizenship (1935), 32; *see also* Nuremberg Laws
lawyers, Jewish, 33
League of Nations, 47
Leiden, 84
Lemkin, Raphael, 2, 19, 89
Liebeskind, Dolek, 71
Lisbon, 51
Lithuania, 1, 57, 70; and assistance to *Einsatzgruppen*, 75; Jews escape through, 51; *see also* Baltic states
London, 78
Lublin, 31, 50; ghetto liquidated, 60; Jews deported from, 65, 104; *Judenrat* in, 69
Luxembourg, 1; *see also* Benelux countries
Luxemburg, Rosa, 22
Lwów, 104; ghetto liquidated, 60, 99
Łódź, 53, 68, 104; *Judenrat*, 68, 107; mortality in ghetto, 95

Macedonia, 72
Madagascar, 31, 50
Majdanek, 57, 58, 104
Marxism: represented as Jewish doctrine, 22–3
Mauthausen, 58

medical experiments, 59
Mein Kampf, 15, 22, 41, 64
mentally retarded, 2
Merin, Moshe, 68
Minsk, 54, 69, 70
Mischling, 33
Munich, 34

Napoleon, 11
nationalism, Jewish, 12; *see also* Zionism, Zionists
National Socialism, *see* Nazism
Nazi Party, 14; anti-Jewish rhetoric of, 20–1; and elections, 20, 23; programme of, 28
Nazism, 17–18, 90; 'historicization' of, 26
Netherlands (Holland), 1, 59, 66, 84; takes in *St Louis* refugees, 49; *see also* Benelux countries
Neumann, Franz, 18, 19
newspapers, Jewish, 39
Nisko, 50, 63
Norway, 1, 35, 59, 73, 76; and deportation of Jews, 72
Nuremberg, 34
Nuremberg Laws, 21, 32, 33, 40; Jewish assessments of, 91–2

Occupied Eastern Territories, Ministry of, 20
Operation Reinhard, 60
Organization of Independent Orthodox Communities, 40

Palestine, 44–8, 51, 94; immigration restricted, 79
partisans, 71
Płaszów, 59
Poland, 1, 11, 24, 30, 33, 35, 49, 51, 52, 53, 56, 59, 60, 63, 65, 66, 71, 75, 81, 91; eastern, 57; interwar, 12, 64; *see also* Jews in Poland; Poles
Poles, 2, 3, 12–13, 19, 20; distinguished from Jews by Nazis, 20;

and killing of Jews, 75–6; situation compared to Jews, 95
Poliakov, Léon, 28
police: French, 59; German, 24, 57; Jewish ghetto, 75; Polish, 75
Polish government-in-exile, 65; and killing of Jews, 75–6; asked to assist Jews, 105, 109–10
Polish underground, 62, 65, 109–10; and killing of Jews, 75–6; reports on condition of Jews, 95; reports on liquidation of Warsaw ghetto, 100–1
Ponary, 102, 103
Portugal, 51
Poznań speech (Himmler), 83, 110
Prague, 51; Jewish Emigration Office in, 36
Pridham, Geoffrey, 20
Protectorate of Bohemia and Moravia, *see* Bohemia and Moravia, Protectorate of

Race, in Hitler's world-view, 15–16
Radom, 104
Rauschning, Hermann, 18, 19, 90
Reform Jews, 11
Reformation, 24
Refugees, Jewish, 48–9; Evian Conference on, 48; Bermuda Conference on, 78
Regat, 73
Reich Labour Service, 25
Reich Main Security Office (RSHA), 59
Reichmann, Eva G., 94
Reichsvereinigung der Juden in Deutschland, 48, 66
Reichsvertretung der deutschen Juden, 43, 48, 92; Zionists join, 45
'resettlement', 61
resistance: spiritual, 44; Allied governments and, 78; armed,

70–1; voluntary communal institutions and, 69
Rhein valley, 8, 10
Ribbentrop, Joachim von, 91
Riga, 54
'righteous gentiles', 77
Ringelblum, Emmanuel, 65
Roma, 1, 3, 55; *see also* Gypsies
Romania, Romanians, 1, 12, 35, 49, 60, 76, 79; Jews in, 13, 49; and killing of Jews, 73–4; loses territory to Hungary, 74
Roosevelt, Franklin, 48, 62
RSHA, 59
Rumkowski, M.H., 68; speaks to Łódź ghetto, 107
Russia, 11; *see also* Soviet Union

SA, 39
Sachsenhausen, 58
'salvation through work', 68–70, 106–7
Schindler, Oskar, 77
Second World War, 30
Sefardic, *see* Jews
'selection', 59
self-help, 69, 108
Serbia, Serbs, 35, 60, 73; *see also* Yugoslavia
Shanghai, 51
Shirer, W.L., 41
Siberia, 53, 54
Sinti, 1, 3, 55; *see also* Gypsies
Slavs, 2, 3, 19, 56
Slovakia, 35, 60, 76; deportation of Jews from, 60, 73
Sobibór, 57, 58, 60
socialists, 22
Solmssen, Georg, 40
Sonderkommando, 59, 99–100
Soviet Union, 1, 35, 36, 50, 51, 53, 55, 56, 57, 59, 64, 70, 73, 75, 78, 86, 98–9; *see also* Jews in the Soviet Union
SS, 59, 63, 83
'stab-in-the-back', 22

Stanisławów, 104
Star of David: Jews ordered to wear, 34; marks Jewish-owned shops, 44
St Louis, 49
storm troopers, *see* SA
Sweden, 72, 79
synagogues: destroyed, 34

T4, 55, 56
Tarnopol, 104
Tarnów, 104
Third Reich, 1; foreign policy of, 36; formulating Jewish policy in, 29–31
Thrace, 72
Transnistria, 73–4; proposal to release Jews from, 78
Trans-Siberian railroad, 51
Trawniki, 59
Treblinka, 57, 58, 60
Turkey, 3

Ukrainians, 19; and killing of Jews, 75
Union Générale des Israélites de France, 66
United States, 48, 49, 55, 105; Jews in, 12; War Department, 2
Upper Silesia, 68
USSR, *see* Soviet Union
Ustaše, 73

Vatican, 74
Versailles Treaty, 36
veterans, Jewish, 39
Vienna, 16, 51; Hungarian Jews marched towards, 74; Jewish Emigration Office in, 36; Jews deported to Nisko, 50; violence against Jews: in the ancient world, 8; in the Middle Ages, 9–10; in Nazi Germany, 34, 39
Volk, Völker, 15
Volkswart, 29

Wallenberg, Raoul, 79
Wannsee Conference, 56, 57, 58, 59, 60, 72, 97
War Refugee Board, 79
Warsaw, 52, 53, 63, 65, 76, 104–6, 108; armed resistance in, 67–9; ghetto established, 95; ghetto liquidated, 60, 100–1; *Judenrat*, 67–9, 105–6;
Warthegau, 104
Washington, DC, 78
Wasserstein, Bernard, 78
Weimar Republic, 22, 23
Wetzel, Erhard, 19, 20
Wilno, 64, 68, 70, 102, 103, 104
Winter Aid, 42
Wippermann, Wolfgang, 55

women, Jewish: and emigration, 42; respond to persecution, 40
Yad Vashem, 77
Yiddish, 10, 12
youth movements: as alternative ghetto leadership, 70; in ghettos, 65; in interwar Poland, 64
Yugoslavia, 1; Italian-occupied regions of, 72; loses territory to Hungary, 74; *see also* Croatia; Serbia

Zionism, Zionists, 12, 44–6, 64, 94
Złoczów, 104
Zygielbojm, Szmul, 105
Zyklon B, 58
Żegota (Council for Aid to Jews), 75, 77, 109–10